Theology
and the
Human Spirit

Theology and the Human Spirit

Essays in Honor of Perry D. LeFevre

Edited by
Theodore W. Jennings and Susan Brooks Thistlethwaite

Exploration Press
Chicago, Illinois

Studies in Ministry and Parish Life

Exploration Press
Chicago Theological Seminary
5757 University Avenue
Chicago, Illinois 60637

ISBN: 0-913552-48-8

Library of Congress Catalog Card Number: 92-73228

Table of Contents

Preface, From a Colleague, *Philip A. Anderson*..3
Introduction, *Susan Brooks Thistlethwaite* and *Theodore W. Jennings*.................9

Part I
Theology: In Relation to God We Speak in Order to Listen

Chapter I   The Idea of a Liberal Christian Theological Seminary,
W. Widick Schroeder..13

Chapter II   To Imagine A World: Constructive Theology,
Susan Brooks Thistlethwaite 27

Chapter III   Theological Anthropology, *Theodore W. Jennings* 35

Chapter IV   Left-Handed Prayer, *W. Dow Edgerton* 45

Part II
Human Development: Since God is Everywhere,
Listen to the Language of Events and Relationships

Chapter V   The American Chalk Circle: Whose Child is This?
Bonnie J. Miller-McLemore 57

Chapter VI   Joseph Son of Jacob, *André LaCocque* 69

Chapter VII   The Perfidy of Corban, *Graydon F. Snyder* 83

Part III
Theological Education: In Relation to Our Fellow Human Beings,
We Listen in Order to Speak, To Give Testimony

Chapter VIII The Christian Teacher, Then and Now, *Dorothy C. Bass*........91

Chapter IX   The Appropriate Use of Research in the Doctor of
Ministry Program, *William R. Myers* 99

Chapter X   Thoughts on a Praxis of Transformative Education,
George F. Cairns 107

Notes about the Contributors 119
Publications by Perry D. LeFevre 121

Theology and the Human Spirit

Preface

The preface is the manuscript of an oral presentation Philip A. Anderson delivered at a dinner honoring Perry LeFevre

From a Colleague

by Philip A. Anderson

Perry, I bring you greetings from two former presidents under whom you served. Last week when I told Cush McGiffert I was coming to your retirement party, he said, "Retirement is a little suicide." He will be one hundred years old in November and keeps *doing*, publishing two books this year. He sends you his latest entitled *Anecdotage*. Ed Manthei, on the other hand represents the *being* side of retirement. He says just *be*. He no longer writes, or prays, or preaches (though he still hasn't thrown out his last two boxes of sermons). He gardens a little, enjoys TV and his neighbors. So there you have it, Doing or Being. And greetings from Cush and Ed. They remember you with great appreciation.

In doing research for this reflection I decided to find out what was going on in the world at critical points in the LeFevre history.

In 1921 a national quota system was applied to immigration. The Unknown Soldier was interred at Arlington. Picasso painted Three Musicians. The U.S. population was 107 million. The "shimmy" is condemned by the Catholic Archbishop of Ohio.

And Perry LeFevre is born in New Paltz, N.Y. A lot has happened in seventy years, and this could be a long evening.

1939: The U.S. recognizes the Franco government. Einstein writes FDR, warning of the possibility of atomic weapons. Italy invades Albania, Germany invades Poland, Steinbeck publishes Grapes of Wrath.

Perry LeFevre enters Harvard College.

1943: Warsaw ghetto uprising. US war contractors barred from racial discrimination. Race riots in Detroit kill thirty four. US troops invade Italy. Hemingway publishes For Whom the Bell Tolls.

Perry LeFevre enters CTS and comes early during the summer in order to case the joint. One reason he chose CTS was his reading of an article by Sam Kincheloe on the behavior sequence of a dying church. Perry was impressed.

One September afternoon in this year 1943 Perry invited another new student to his fourth floor room for tea and thus began the education of Phil Anderson by this wise man from the East. Tea was an education. I was a Swede from Minnesota who drank coffee. I'm not sure I had ever tasted tea. And some of his Harvard language was fresh — words like "crud" for whatever we had to eat and "sewer trout" for fish he didn't like. Not all education goes on in the classroom. The tea parties continued and others joined us: Jim Smucker, Roy Wiebe, Al Edyvean, Graham Waring. We also began creating a lot of second hand smoke with our pipes. In those sexist days I used to send my laundry home and when it came back it always had raisin cake or cookies or good crud in it from my mother. Perry had a way of knowing what mail had arrived, and he would come to my room shortly afterwards wondering what was in my laundry. The fourth floor tea and education party was off and running.

1945: Yalta conference. U.S. forces invade Iwo Jima and Okinawa. Roosevelt dies. Truman president. Auschwitz and Buchenwald liberated. Germany surrenders. Atomic bombs dropped. Airplane hits Empire State building killing thirteen.

Perry LeFevre starts attending Bond Chapel in the Divinity School. The fourth floor tea irregulars took note of this unusual behavior. Finally I went over one day myself. The reason for Perry's new behavior was singing soprano in the choir: a beautiful person with a voice to match, who changed her name to Carol LeFevre the following year.

Many of you are familiar with one of my favorite sayings: "It is easier to act your way into a new way of thinking than to think your way into a new way of acting." Perry's new behavior in going to Bond Chapel has always puzzled me. He just may be the exception to my rule. He thought himself into that new behavior.

1946: First session of the U.N. Philippine independence. Strikes. Churchill's Iron Curtain speech. Spock Baby and Child Care book. Chester Carlson receives patent for "xerography" Unfortunately the fourth floor members of the tea party didn't have the money or the sense to buy Xerox stock.

Perry and I were ordained in a double ordination service in Graham Taylor Hall, the same week we graduated from CTS and the Federated Theological Faculty. Both of us had seen the "more light" which is yet to break forth from God's word. Perry left the Reformed Church and I left the Swedish Evangelical Mission Covenant church to become Congregationalists. In August Phoebe and I were married. In September Perry and Carol were married.

1953: Korean armistice. Earl Warren appointed Chief Justice. Skinner writes Science and Human Behavior. Watson and Crick show that the structure of DNA is a double helix. Pope Pius XII disapproves of psychoanalysis.

Perry LeFevre is called to the faculty of Chicago Theological Seminary and the Federated Faculty of the University of Chicago. After leaving CTS and Chicago Perry had studied at Cambridge in England, Union in New York, taught at Franklin and Marshal and Knox colleges, and earned the Ph.D. from the University of Chicago in 1951.

Carol and Perry bought a row house at 5220 Greenwood Ave. and here one of Perry's skills which the Seminary never really capitalized on appeared: his ability to fix things with very little money. They renovated that old house and moved in with their three children, Suzy, Judy and Peter. Our families grew up together. If Perry had been business manager of CTS he would have balanced the budget. But he couldn't do everything, even though he did win a Kaiser automobile in a national contest by writing twenty-five words or less about how to make democracy live.

1954: The Supreme Court strikes down separate but equal. Joe McCarthy has his TV hearings on communist influence. Senate condemns McCarthy. Williams writes Cat on a Hot Tin Roof.

Perry moves into the fifth floor tower office from which he is now trying to extricate himself. It is widely rumored and probably true that the idea for the comic strip SHOE by Jeff MacNelly came from a visit to Perry's office in its heyday. Over these thirty eight years that office has been one of the seminary attractions and tourist stopping places. I often took my visitors up there after the cloisters and the chapels. His office never failed to impress people.

I had joined the faculty in 1954. The tea party was reinstated after an eight year hiatus, moving from the fourth to the fifth floor tower — the longest running tea party in the western hemisphere.

Over the years Perry's office has been a treasure and treacherous for me. As you know the filing system was vertical. Filing cabinets often had the drawers hanging open with little or nothing in them. But the floor was covered with stacks of papers, file folders and books. One pile was trust, another theological education, the course and potential book of spirituality, faculty minutes, CTS correspondence. Some piles, of course, became covered with dust and forgotten. NO. During tea some subject would come up and Perry could go unerringly to a dusty pile and pull out the correspondence or old faculty minutes pertaining to the subject at hand. Amazing. And I figured he didn't have to be cleanly about it (the custodians always gave the office a wide berth). There was only a little passageway that could be swept and no surface clear enough to be dusted. If cleanliness is next to Godliness, Perry was nearer to God on the fifth floor than anyone else at CTS so he let the cleanliness go.

About a year ago something changed. I was in his office and he wanted a paper and he could not find it in all the piles. It was like a recent SHOE comic strip in which Shoe says "I knew it would happen some day" and in the second picture his desk has fallen over and he says "My data base has crashed." I figured retirement was around the corner or down the steps.

1960: Gary Powers captured after his spy plane was shot down over the Soviet Union. Eichmann arrested and brought to Israel for trial. Krushchev bangs shoe at the UN. Sit-ins in Greensboro, N.C. First laser produced.

Perry LeFevre becomes the Academic Dean of the Chicago Theological Seminary as it re-establishes itself after the end of the Federated Theological Faculty. For twenty years he was Dean leading the faculty as it created a new curriculum, recruited new faculty members, and developed innovative programs. Perry increasingly provided continuity at CTS for thirty nine years, serving with six presidents: McGiffert, Schomer, Manthei, Campbell, Rooks and Smith, and two acting Presidents, Reneker and Obenhaus. Perry, I salute you for your being which allowed you to live productively with eight presidential styles, many more faculty idiosyncrasies, and myriad student demands and counterdemands. Through all of these years you remained an incredibly steady presence and leader. I never heard a word of complaint, maybe a mumbling word of frustration now and then which would become negotiated over time.

How did you do it? I want to lift up and celebrate the marks of your leadership and teaching style. They are not hard to find for in a remarkable manner you practiced what you taught.

LISTEN. In June 1985 you charged the graduating class with this one word, and added that "I have come to believe that the central meaning of the religious life could be expressed in that one word: LISTEN." You elaborated on that word in your address at the Winter 1988 convocation. You went on to say, "Listen for the word of God, in the Prime Testament and the New Testament, but since God is interwoven in the very fabric of life, and since God is everywhere, listen to the language of events and relationships." "Prayer begins in earnest when we stop talking and begin to listen. Prayer may begin with words, but if we speak, we speak in order to listen," and finally your dictum: "In relation to God we speak in order to listen; in relation to our fellow human beings we listen in order to speak, to give testimony."

You did listen, to all of us, from President to students to staff, to faculty, to me. Embedded in your listening was a great caring for persons. You were non-judgemental.

Occasionally, you would call me up after a long listening session with someone. We would drink tea and you would puzzle about why the person stayed so long, going over the same story. Yet to my knowledge you never hurried anyone, unless you really did have a meeting.

The second word that has characterized your style is FAIRNESS and this includes support and encouragement of everyone — students, faculty, administration. Even persons who held different viewpoints, you treated fairly. I can recall the occasional times when I had strong feelings about some issue or person, you never jumped on my bandwagon. You heard me. And in the course of time things got worked out.

I believe your support of creativity and innovation has been a great boon to CTS. One experience of my own will illustrate this style of yours which contrasted so dramatically with other institutions.

I remember a pastoral care professor from another seminary telling of the struggle he had in the late sixties to get a rug on the floor of a classroom. He wanted some freedom beyond desks and chairs in rows to let students move around, meditate, do yoga, sit on the floor, which radically changes your perception of a situation. He struggled for more than 6 months going through dean, president, finally arguing his case before the Board of Directors, and split vote in order to get that rug. Then he took a lot of flak from his colleagues. As I listened I was aware that CTS already had a rug on the floor in 450. I had gone to Perry two years earlier saying I wanted a rug on the floor and he asked "In which room?" He trusted me as he trusted all of us. If I wanted a rug, O.K.

Fairness leads to a third word, CONSENSUS. I can still recall new members of the faculty asking, "When do we vote?" During your 20 years in the deanship, you relied on a process that allowed consensus to develop. We maybe voted five times. And CTS was the stronger for it, not racked by divisions and infighting. When I asked Ed Manthei for words which he would apply to your leadership, he added "patience and tolerance" which allowed the process to work. Out of your listening, in meetings you could find threads of common agreement, strands of shared beliefs out of which a consensus we could all support would emerge. And you did this for myriad cluster committees as well.

CREATIVITY is the fourth word. You had ideas about curriculum, D.Min. projects, the suburban project in which students lived in different places and studied there. The Kenwood project which related students to various gangs and projects in Kenwood and Woodlawn, and tragically shut down after Martin Luther King was assassinated. Your pedagogical creativity in the new curriculum of 1960, enabling CTS to be a leader in innovation, recognized by the ATS. Our D. Rel. program, an early innovation which merged into the D.Min. nomenclature. I still hear from D. Rel. students from the late 60's about the formative influence that program had on their ministry.

Your ability has been recognized by the ATS and the North Central Association. You have been on more accrediting teams to other seminaries than all the rest of the faculty combined. Your listening, fairness and track record here at CTS have made you a valued visitor to dozens of other schools.

The final word is THEOLOGIAN. Undergirding all of your leadership is your central theological convictions which are best expressed in your own words, "that whatever makes movement possible for a person toward becoming a center of freedom and love is ultimately trustworthy . . . and whatever it is that creates centers of freedom and love in human life is God for women and men. Whatever heals the inner conflict of the divided self and releases a person from bondage to self and to the past, whatever overcomes hostility and answers the loneliness of persons, healing the brokenness between persons, this reality alone can be finally trusted. This is creation and redemption of a transcendence that heals and saves, and that creates new good."

Perry, you have been for all of us a wise friend and teacher from the East, enabling us on our journeys toward becoming centers of freedom and love. You have played a great part in making CTS that kind of center for persons and I can hardly imagine CTS without you. Footnote: As you leave that fifth floor office be sure to pick up the pile of papers on the floor marked trust, and go home and finish the book. The world needs that book. And don't forget the tea pot.

Introduction

by Theodore W. Jennings and Susan Brooks Thistlethwaite

Phil Anderson, colleague and friend, emphasizes that for Perry LeFevre listening is the central meaning of religious life. We have divided the contributions to this *festschrift* into the dimensions of listening that Anderson elaborates: I. Theology: In Relation to God We Speak in Order to Listen; II. Human Development: Since God is Everywhere, Listen to the Language of Events and Relationships; III. Theological Education: In Relation to our Fellow Human Beings, We Listen in Order to Speak, to Give Testimony.

The theology section begins with Widick Schroeder's intellectual history of the forces that gave birth to this particular kind of a seminary...... Schroeder recalls us to the foundational liberal commitment to the fostering of genuine pluralism of perspective and "freedom of inquiry and debate which is at the heart of a liberal seminary."

Susan Thistlethwaite continues this section by describing the trajectory in the teaching of theology at CTS from Constructive to Liberation. While there are distinctions and even tensions between the two, what unites them is LeFevre's and Thistlethwaite's emphasis on theological anthropology, the necessity for community of dialogue in order for theology to be done.

Ted Jennings elaborates the necessity, as posited by LeFevre, "to understand humanity in the light of the insights of the Christian Tradition." Post-modernism has initiated a sea change in our understanding of culture and society; we seem to be many human beings, not just the unitary "man." The press toward the actualization of the 'not yet fully human' may provide a way to talk about humanity in the midst of pluralism.

When the present seems fragmentary and the future uncertain, on what can we rely, or, as Dow Edgerton poses a key preoccupation of Perry LeFevre's work, "What can we trust?" Prayer, even the prayer of emptiness, becomes, especially in the form of public prayer, the means for trusting to occur. "Teach me to pray, I pray."

In Part II, we note that for Perry LeFevre one of the most generative of conversation partners for the theologian has been the field of psychology. Understanding the human must involve a depth perception of the stages of human life and a sense of how human community evolves through these stages in each culture. As Bonnie Miller-McLemore points out, the narrowed place for "child" in recent times in the U.S. has serious theological consequences. New forms of family do not preclude healthy human psychological development, but for healthy development to occur, care for the child must become more central that it currently is. After all, this is where we begin in the task of becoming human.

Both Andre LaCocque and Graydon Snyder carry through the theme of human development and community. Surely the parent-child relationship, echoing Miller-McLemore, is the most formative of human attachments, as LaCocque's essay testifies. The movement from child to adult to older adult also involves displacement which occurs in the aging process, notes Snyder.

In Part III are chapters that underline that the act of becoming human is not to be left to chance. The work of the theological educator is to assist in this task through educational method. But not all have agreed, observes Dorothy Bass, that Jerusalem should have a lot to do with Athens. Teaching and Christian faith have much to do with each other, however, especially as presented by Perry LeFevre in *The Christian Teacher* (1958). The need for personal vocation, existential commitment and divine purpose is as great today as in 1958.

Basic to LeFevre's theological anthropology is his conviction that human life can yield values and meanings which can be identified, nurtured and *sustained* to counter the evils in existence. Concretely, how does this occur in ministry?

Research methods in the Doctor of Ministry program at CTS, writes William Myers, can operate to reveal empirical forces at work in ministry, but only if the method is carefully chosen to be congruent with the values of both researcher and subject.

Personal and social transformation occurs when the educational process enables the student, according to George Cairns, to become "more fully human." Human community, the basis of both personal and social transformation, then becomes possible.

This collection of essays, while markedly diverse in some ways, does testify to an enduring vision: human beings are a way God is known, human community is possible and transformation in the direction of an increase of value in the world can occur.

The question is not, therefore, only whether to be or not to be, but what to *become*. The life work of Perry LeFevre is an exploration of this task of human becoming. He is a cartographer of the human landscape. We hope that we have used well the maps he has provided us.

Teach me to listen, I pray
Teach me to speak, I pray
Teach me to pray, I pray

Part I

THEOLOGY

In Relation to God We Speak in Order to Listen

CHAPTER I

The Idea of a Liberal Christian Theological Seminary

by W. Widick Schroeder

INTRODUCTION

The editors of this volume have invited present and some former faculty members of the Chicago Theological Seminary to contribute essays to this Festschrift honoring Perry LeFevre, Professor of Constructive Theology, on the occasion of his retirement. He has served on its faculty with great distinction for thirty-one years. He was also academic dean of the seminary for the first twenty years of its reconstitution as a separate school following the dissolution of the Federated Theological Faculty of the University of Chicago in 1961. In this role, he made major contributions to the theory guiding the organization of the seminary's curriculum and to its embodiment in a program of study.

The chapter titles of this volume reveal the broad range of issues faculty members have addressed and the diversity of interpretive frameworks they have employed. LeFevre embraced this variety with enthusiasm, for he sought faculty people who were both able scholars and who held contrasting theological interpretations. In pursuing these objectives, he was informed by a cluster of foundational liberal values which will be addressed in this essay. Some aspects of this discussion are idiosyncratic to this particular institution, but many of the issues considered here emerge in most liberal Protestant theological seminaries in the United States in this historical epoch.[1]

This essay examines the liberal heritage enmeshed in the history of this Christian theological seminary. In this context it explores both specialized secondary forms of liberalism and the foundational liberal values which are intertwined with them. In addition, it addresses the implications of foundational liberal values for the life of a liberal Christian theological seminary. If such a seminary is to survive with integrity, most students, faculty, administrative officers, members of its Board of Trustees and members of its broader constituencies must share a basic commitment to these foundational liberal values.

THE LIBERAL HERITAGE

As noted in the introduction, Perry LeFevre, both as an administrator and as a professor, is strongly committed to the foundational liberal ideas. He incorporates these inclusive ideas within a more specialized form of liberalism associated with one facet of the history of this institution. It is necessary to retrieve selected aspects of this history in order to understand better the current situation.

The Social Gospel movement, though informed in part by the specialized theological liberalism of nineteenth century German Protestant thought (particularly the anti-metaphysical thought of Albrecht Ritschl), was an indigenous American movement in theology. It emerged in the latter part of the nineteenth century and flowered in the early decades of the twentieth century. Its influence was widespread in several American denominations, including the Congregational churches associated with the Chicago Theological Seminary and the Baptist churches associated with the Divinity School of the University of Chicago. During the first three or four decades of the twentieth century both of these institutions attracted numerous faculty who were leaders in that movement and many students who were broadly sympathetic to it. They were very concerned with social justice issues, and many envisioned the progressive embodiment of a love ethic in the social order. Skeptical about the validity of ontological and metaphysical analyses, the proponents of this movement sought to utilize the emerging human sciences, especially sociology and psychology, to further the "Christianizing" of the social order. They entertained a relatively optimistic view of human nature and focused their theological interpretations on the life and teachings of Jesus of Nazareth. In their selective abstraction from the Biblical records, they developed a social ethic of love modeled after Jesus' life and teachings. They promoted a love ethic as a basis both for personal conduct and for the progressive transformation of the social order. They hoped that persuasion, harmony and equality would reduce or eliminate coercion, conflict, and injustice in the social order.

By the time Perry LeFevre arrived at the seminary as a student in 1943, the Social Gospel was under serious attack and its direct influence in liberal American theological institutions was in decline. The radical neo-orthodoxy of Karl Barth which developed in Europe after the first world war and the more moderate neo-orthodoxy of Reinhold Niebuhr which evolved in the United States during the 1930s, coupled with the Great Depression and World War II, led many to challenge the theological assumptions informing this specialized form of theological liberalism. People assailed it, claiming it was excessively confident about the goodness of human nature, was unduly optimistic about social progress, and was theologically shallow.

In the Chicago context, people associated with the Social Gospel form of theological liberalism began to explore alternative philosophical and theological moorings for their interpretations of the Christian movement. In the 1930s

Henry Nelson Wieman in the Divinity School and Charles Hartshorne in the philosophy department of the University of Chicago led the quest for the development of new forms of theological liberalism. In the 1930s and 1940s members of the "Chicago School" utilized the resources of the pragmatism of John Dewey and William James, the emergent evolution of Henri Bergson, the interaction social psychology of George Herbert Mead, the value theory of Ralph Barton Perry and, above all, the philosophy of Alfred North Whitehead in their work. In the late 1930s and early 1940s Bernard Meland, Bernard Loomer and Daniel Day Williams joined Wieman and Hartshorne in the development of neo-liberal thought, elaborating richer and more complex interpretations of the Christian movement than those associated with the Social Gospel.

By the time Perry LeFevre matriculated at CTS, this neo-liberal movement of thought was a major factor in the Chicago complex.[2] The scholars just noted were central to the early development of what subsequently has been called process theology. As one would expect in the development of any rich theological movement,"family quarrels" and contrasting emphases developed among the initiators of this theological and philosophical movement. Three strands of process theology, expressing contrasting views of the status of human reason and its relation to experience, have developed. Further, these cited people differed in the attention they gave to Christian beliefs, doctrines and practices in their constructive work. Because these contrasting emphases and understandings illumine the context stimulating LeFevre's early work, it is fitting to sketch the contrasts between these initiators of process theology and to locate LeFevre's work within this group.

Wieman and Hartshorne, both in Whitehead's debt, accentuated different facets of his thought and held contrasting views about the status of reason and its ability to illumine the nature of things. Whitehead himself emphasized both rational and empirical factors in the development of speculative philosophy. Coherence and logic were the rational criteria; applicability and adequacy were the empirical criteria. Because adequacy entailed the applicability of the schematism to all occasions, it is necessary. This necessity tied the rational and empirical sides of the schematism together.

Whitehead's faith in rationalism was grounded on a transrational intuition that there was a relational matrix inherent in the nature of things which reason could penetrate. Limitations of insight and of language precluded the development of a fully adequate metaphysics, but progress was possible. Because the ultimate of ultimates for Whitehead was a creativity beyond forms, the ultimacy of that creativity could be shown only by an appeal to intuition. Further, eternal objects (comparable to the Platonic forms) constituted a multiplicity, but they were not a class. One could not, therefore, be led to a vision of the Good, the transformal form at the base of things, by the proper use of the dialectic, as Plato maintained in *The Republic*. Consequently, reason played an important but not an unqualified role in illumining the nature of things. In his philosophical writings, Whitehead maintained a careful balance between the rational and empirical facets of his work.

While Whitehead held that the Divine Reality served as the principle of order, the locus of potentiality, and the mediator of experience from one creature to another and was the ultimate receptor of all that had become, he refused to advance proofs for the existence of God. Instead, he simply explored the implications of his metaphysics for the Divine Reality, which was the supreme exemplification of metaphysical propositions.

Wieman rejected some facets of Whitehead's philosophy as too speculative and focused on the empirical side of things. Hartshorne strongly emphasized the more rational side of Whitehead's philosophy and was less restrained about the limits of reason than was he.

Consequently, three strands of process thinking have emerged in the past several decades. Perry LeFevre, Bernard Loomer and Bernard Meland have minimized the speculative side of Whitehead and are more closely identified with Wieman. Others, such as John Cobb, Daniel Day Williams, David Ray Griffin, Marjorie Suchocki, William Christian and Lewis Ford, are seeking to maintain the balance between the rational and empirical sides of Whitehead's philosophy and are more closely identified with Whitehead himself. Still others, such as Schubert Ogden, David Tracy and Franklin I. Gamwell, have accentuated the rational side of Whitehead's philosophy and are more closely identified with Hartshorne. LeFevre, Meland, Cobb, Williams, Griffin, Suchocki, Ogden and Tracy have focused more explicitly on the Christian movement in their work, but all are interested in the relation of their work to other fields.

THE TWO MEANINGS OF LIBERALISM

In the preceding section, the Social Gospel and neo-liberalism, two specialized forms of theological liberalism, were noted. Both of these specialized forms contain generic liberal ideas more inclusive than those embodied in these particular species. At its foundational level Christian liberalism is a mode of thought requiring a methodological commitment to free and open inquiry and debate into the beliefs and practices embodied in the Christian movement. It does not entail a commitment to a particular set of beliefs and practices.

The seventeenth and eighteenth century movement of European thought known as the Enlightenment and nineteenth century English liberalism contributed greatly to these ideas. The Enlightenment also played a major role in legitimating human rights, religious liberty, religious pluralism, and religious freedom, ideas which are also part of the fundamental liberal values informing the institutional basis of this liberal Christian theological seminary. In these days when in some theological circles Europhobia is widespread and the ideas of the Enlightenment and/or nineteenth century English liberalism are widely criticized for the shallowness of their rationalism and their excessively individualistic view of human nature, the contributions of these movements of thought to the core matrix of ideas sustaining a liberal Christian theological seminary need to be reaffirmed.

While sharing these core values with a substantial majority of persons associated with modern Western universities, Christian liberalism has a more focused subject matter — the beliefs, feelings, and practices associated with the Christian movement.

Writing fifty years ago, the late Daniel Day Williams, a CTS alumnus, for many years a member of the seminary faculty, and a leading proponent of one form of process theology, expressed his understanding of the foundational meaning of Christian liberalism in this way:

> Christian theology is an inquiry for the correct expression of those truths which are discovered within the Christian movement and which can be expressed in Christian symbols. It arises within the Christian movement and is organically related to it as its frame of reference. Thus it is to the Christian movement as a whole, in all its breadth and depth and ramifications, that theology belongs; but no presuppositions about the absolute or supernatural character of any portion of the beliefs or objects of the movement need be accepted as the starting-point. The theologian may legitimately inquire as to the truth of any proposition which appears within the Christian fold, and the nature and significance of Christianity itself 'may be a legitimate object of theological inquiry.[3]

Williams goes on to suggest some propositions with which a Christian might agree, such as "The Christian movement offers a significant body of experience and idea related to the objects of religion; it is therefore worthy of exploration" or "Somewhere within the Christian movement there are significant clues to truth." Acknowledging that such beliefs are not the beliefs of all Christians, Williams notes that they constitute the "... most general judgments of importance and relevance which theology, like any inquiry, must make about its subject matter."[4]

He then elaborates a view which is primary for the liberal Christian view:

> The plain fact is that there is no one set of propositions about any of the objects of Christian concern or about the method of Christian thinking which all Christian churches are agreed upon. In the creedal churches, apart from Rome, interpretation of the creeds is left to the individual. Further, the basis on which the creed is believed and recited is not prescribed by the creed itself. Christians do arrive at their beliefs by different routes, and their beliefs differ. How then can any one starting-point and any one theological method be prescribed for Christian thought?...No Christian or church can prescribe any dogma which is not open to Christian inquiry and revision in the light of the truth which the Christian movement has always professed to seek.[5]

While Daniel Day Williams and Perry LeFevre have both used notions drawn from facets of pragmatism and process theology to interpret key Christian doctrines and practices, neither insists these modes of thought — or any other specialized mode of thought — should be imposed upon one who is seeking to discern the truth of Christian doctrine and practice.

In this spirit, the Chicago Theological Seminary has been open to students of all denominations and of no denomination and has freely called scholars to its faculty who do not share the more specialized forms of theological liberalism of people such as Williams and LeFevre. The institution requires no confessional or creedal commitment from its faculty or its students. Neither an orthodoxy nor an orthopraxis is a criterion for admission to its student body or appointment to its faculty. Members of the community are free to explore the Christian movement and other religious and secular movements without any *a priori* restrictions or limitations, other than seriousness of intent and responsible intellectual work. Attesting to the depth of the seminary's commitment to these principles, only a minority of the students and of the faculty as it is presently constituted are affiliated with the United Church of Christ, its primary supporting denomination.

Tensions are greatest when persons in the seminary community insist their way of doing theology is *the* way theology must be done and/or affirm that their understanding of social ethics and the public policy implications of their views should become institutional policy. The community can sustain some people in its midst who entertain such monolithic views; but if one such view were to become dominant, the liberal idea informing the institution would be in serious trouble.

This liberal theological institution is grounded on three primary values — tolerance for alternative interpretations of the beliefs and practices of the Christian movement, the legitimacy of theological pluralism in its midst, and the right of participants in the community to pursue freely their own modes of theological inquiry.[6] These fundamental values do not require one to commit oneself either to the particular species of theological liberalism dominant in this school in the first part of this century, forms rooted in the Kantian *Critiques* and/or the thought of the nineteenth century neo-Kantian revisionists and their Social Gospel successors, or to the so-called process theology associated with Alfred North Whitehead and his school. They do require one to commit oneself to sustain an institutional ethos which supports its members as they pursue multiple modes of inquiry informed by any of a variety of metatheories.

While these core values give shape to the understanding of the seminary as an institution, its participants must appropriate a more specialized understanding of the Christian movement into their own work. Their engagements with the Christian heritage and with contemporary theology, ethics, and culture are the matrix out of which such personal convictions emerge. Their encounters with the forms through which ministry is practiced focus their professional understandings. Students have access to the faculties of the seminary, other theological institutions in the area, and the University of Chicago. As seminary students struggle to develop constructive theological viewpoints which they can maintain with spiritual, intellectual and emotional integrity, they can utilize these immense resources. Because of the liberal interest in both Christian and non-Christian modes of thought and also in the universality of the faith entailed in the *Logos* doctrine, liberal Christian seminaries are enriched by close proximity to major universities. The Chicago Theological Seminary is extremely fortunate in this regard, for it is adjacent to the University of Chicago, one of the great research universities of our epoch.

Because the seminary is not a creedal, confessing and/or committed community espousing particular Christian beliefs, rituals or practices, it is at most an amorphous or formless church. Members of the seminary community may participate in churches and those in the Believers Church tradition may choose to form churches emerging from the relations they develop in the seminary. However no member of the seminary community is required to participate in a particular community of faith.

THE IMPLICATIONS OF FOUNDATIONAL LIBERAL VALUES
FOR THE LIFE OF A LIBERAL CHRISTIAN SEMINARY

Thus far this essay has explored the relation between the primary liberal values shaping the self-understanding of this institution and the secondary liberal values affirmed by some of its participants. It has done so in order to illumine the "orthodoxy" shaping its life. It is also necessary to address Christian practice, exploring the orthopraxis (right conduct) expected of participants in the seminary community and of the seminary's role in promoting a particular understanding of Christian orthopraxis.

Both in the past and in the present many in the seminary community have been deeply concerned about questions of social justice. Presently, various forms of liberation theology are very fashionable in some parts of the Christian movement and also in this seminary. Its proponents strongly emphasize an orthopraxis, accentuate equality as *the* principle of justice, affirm a "preferential option" for some oppressed group or groups, and provide little space for alternative prudential judgments as to the best means to attain a given end.

Just as there has not been a consensus within the Christian movement as a whole about the interpretation of the beliefs and symbols embodied within it, so there has not been a consensus concerning proper action. Participants in the Christian movement disagree about the relation of the Christian community to the civil community; about the nature of justice, power, and love, individually and in their interrelationships; about the implications of Christian beliefs for the rules and regulations of justice within and without the Christian movement; and about the truth of a teleological or a deontological ethic. Further, they disagree about the nature of the historical situation in which they find themselves; about the possibilities of describing normative forms of social organization in the familial, social, economic, political and/or religious spheres and, if they hold it is possible to suggest normative forms, about their structure; about the desirability of particular public policy proposals; and about fitting theories and methods to use in social and psycho/spiritual analyses.

Just as a liberal Christian theological seminary must seek to provide a supportive framework for the exploration of Christian beliefs, it must also seek to provide a supportive framework for the exploration of Christian practices. Insofar as practice is more concrete, more personal and more encompassing than theory, a liberal Christian seminary must impose relatively more limits on interpersonal conduct within the institution than upon the exploration of the theory informing various practices. The principles of respect for the human person and the limitation of practices directly harmful to others — principles endemic to the primary values of liberalism discussed earlier — shape the rules and regulations of justice in interpersonal relations within the seminary community.

In practice, further limits are imposed on the members of liberal Christian theological seminaries. For example, some scriptures and some Christian social ethical teachings condemn homosexual activity, promote patriarchal forms of family organization, and tolerate or legitimate slavery. Many contemporary Christians find at least some of these biblical passages and attendant social teachings very offensive. Others want to affirm at least some of them, teachings which historically have been widespread within the Christian movement.

Some feminists, some homosexuals, and others sympathetic with the rights they affirm are so outraged by some Christian social teachings on homosexual and male-female relations that they contribute to a climate of opinion leading almost all participants to reject soundly certain Christian social teachings. Those members of the Christian movement affirming some historic beliefs and practices relating to homosexuality and patriarchal forms of family organization may find it difficult — if not impossible — to pursue free and open inquiry on these matters in "liberal" seminaries in this historical epoch.

All are offended by historic social teachings on slavery; those few in the Christian movement in our day defending slavery or caste-structured societies would find it even more difficult to pursue their inquiries in the midst of a liberal seminary. Thus the climate of opinion sets informal limits on free and open inquiry and debate, even in a liberal Christian theological seminary.

CONTEMPORARY THREATS TO A LIBERAL CHRISTIAN THEOLOGICAL SEMINARY

The Loci of Pressures for an Institutional Orthopraxis — Biblical fundamentalism (because of its requirements about biblical orthodoxy), Roman Catholicism (because of its ecclesiastical definition of proper Christian doctrine), some specialized forms of Christian liberalism and some African-American religious beliefs (because of their lack of distinction between communities of faith and communities of politics), some forms of confessional Protestantism (because of their demands for commitment to particular interpretations of Christian doctrine), and some forms of liberation theology (because of the centrality of the dialectic of negation and critical theory in their interpretations of proper Christian practice) constitute major challenges to the theory and practice of a liberal Christian theological seminary.

Because of their attraction to persons associated with groups historically related to liberal Christian theological institutions, some specialized forms of Christian liberalism itself, some forms of African-American religious beliefs and some forms of liberation theology pose the most serious intellectual and institutional challenge to liberal Christian theological seminaries in the United States in the current epoch. Only a small number of biblical fundamentalists and confessional Protestants are attracted to liberal Christian seminaries. The sympathetic understanding of Roman Catholic participants of the nature of non-Catholic liberal theological institutions minimizes threats from this group. Hence, people seeking to promote an institutional orthopraxis are drawn largely from those adherents of the first three types which do not make some principled distinction between their community of faith and their community of politics.

People associated with the Social Gospel movement, as observed earlier, sought to Christianize the social order. People in this tradition have frequently sought to have their communities of faith endorse particular public policy proposals and to support particular political programs. Many African-Americans have historically expected their clergy and their churches to "promote the race." African-American clergy have not infrequently run for public office, seeing no contradiction between an ordained clergy status and that of a public officeholder.

Because some people in these two groups may understand the distinction between a seminary and a church and may affirm foundational liberal values for the former institution, they may be willing to tolerate institutional neutrality on most public policy issues. Others, seeing no distinction in principle between a church and/or a denomination and a liberal Christian theological seminary and using the analogical method to legitimate their claims, seek to persuade a seminary to adopt church and/or denominational statements on public policy issues. Still others try to persuade a seminary to adopt their views, seeking to convert it into a confessing congregation.

In the current period, the most consistent and coherent challenges to the idea of a liberal Christian theological seminary come from proponents of some forms of liberation theology. This particular theological movement emerged in Germany after World War II and became a major movement in the 1960s and 1970s. Emphasizing the coalescence of theory and practice in an orthopraxis and incorporating a properly defined orientation on ecological, sexual, social, economic and/or political matters, people in this theological movement frequently desire persons and institutions to take what its proponents envisage to be politically correct stances on public policy issues.

As is the case with all rich theological movements, liberation theology is complex and multi-dimensional. Some species, informed by the Social Gospel movement, may not pose on principle a threat to the idea of a liberal theological school. Other species, informed by the dialectic of negation as a proper mode of social analysis and critical theory as a basis for the coalescence of *theoria* and *praxis* in an orthopraxis (the generic notions cited earlier and associated with the so-called "Frankfurt School" of sociology), constitute a direct threat to that idea. Rooted directly in the thought of Karl Marx and indirectly in the thought of G. W. F. Hegel and expressed most fully today in the thought of Jürgen Habermas, these notions are in direct conflict with the presuppositions of the foundational liberal values which have shaped the life of liberal Christian theological seminaries in the twentieth century. Consequently if one sought with intellectual and emotional integrity to embody the dialectic of negation and critical theory in one's work, one would have to challenge both the primary notions of religious pluralism, religious tolerance and religious liberty informing the intellectual life of liberal seminaries and also the contrast between theoria and praxis legitimating the distinction between a theological seminary as seminary and a particular community of faith and politics.

Liberation theologians employing the dialectic of negation in social analyses discern inherent conflicts between people who on the basis of selected ascribed characteristics are situated in one of two mutually exclusive social groups. They term one polar group the "oppressor" and the other the "oppressed." Liberation theologians differ in the categories they use to place people in particular social groups. However they always use primary categories grounded on one or more ascribed characteristic, such as sex, race, or age, or on social location. If social location is the basis for categorization they employ ethnicity, nationality, social status, social class, political affiliation, and/or religious affiliation in their analyses. Analysts characterize one group — the one they perceive to have the greatest linear power — as the oppressor and the other group — the one they perceive to have the least linear power — as the oppressed. They interpret history as a dynamic struggle between these interest groups leading to a reconfiguration of the social order and some realignment of power relations. The more utopian liberation theologians envisage a future time of greatly enhanced harmony of life with life, once the dialectical process of social struggle has rendered the polar types obsolete in a transformed social order.

Liberation theologians affirming critical theory hold that all social analyses except their own are ideologies designed to mask the self-interest of their designated dominant group. They use critical theory to unmask ideology and to promote proper political action. They insist that the end of analysis in human affairs is action, where *theoria* and *praxis* coalesce. They think proper analysis will lead to an orthodoxy of orthopraxis. In theological contexts, they replace God talk with God walk. They hold that if one does not take a stand for a proposed public policy view or a prescribed course of political action, he or she is taking a stand against it.

When proponents couple critical theory with the dialectic of negation, they undercut a "middle" ground; for they insist one is either for or against them in the struggles for human liberation. They argue that no person or institution can be neutral in these struggles. Unless proponents of species of liberation theology informed by the dialectic of negation and critical theory are willing to make an exception in the case of liberal theological schools, they are bound to seek to politicize these institutions.

Because this exception would violate the intellectual and emotional integrity of one holding such views, others will have to view such concessions as tactical. They must assume that proponents of critical theory and the dialectic of negation want to establish their values as the core beliefs of the institution to which they are related. Persons holding to the primal values of a liberal Christian theological school have no option but to resist them. In this way, the fact that some people believe that the dialectic of negation is correct (even though it may not be inherent in the nature of things) impacts the life of a liberal Christian theological seminary.

It is difficult to know how many American proponents of liberation theologies have appropriated the dialectic of negation and critical theory, for many motifs in American liberation theologies incorporate ideas promoted by the Social Gospel movement. Unless one knows what species of liberation theology a given proponent is advancing, one cannot know whether liberal or neo-Marxist values are primal for that proponent. If the dialectic of negation and critical theory are primary values, the defender of a liberal Christian theological seminary, as noted in the preceding paragraph, must resist efforts to embody those values at the core of the seminary and must affirm the integrity of those liberal values sustaining the institution.

This seminary has consistently resisted efforts from some of its constituencies to take official positions on public policy issues. In so doing, it has been guided — at least implicitly — by core liberal values. These efforts have been made infrequently, for most members have rejected the idea of an institutional orthopraxis, in spite of their strong interests in human rights and issues of social justice.

In fact, the only issue that has found its way to an official body of the seminary since the Vietnam War was a proposal to declare the seminary a nuclear free zone. That proposal, developed in the late 1980s, was voted down by the seminary's Academic Council. There is no way to know whether the proposal would have been adopted by the Board of Trustees had it reached that body. The fact that some faculty, staff, and students developed and promoted such a declaration reveals the uneven embodiment of fundamental liberal ideas among the seminary's primary constituencies.[7]

In the discussion of this proposal, no one explicitly appealed to critical theory or the dialectic of negation to legitimate their position. Some appealed to denominational statements on nuclear war. Others argued that the seminary should be in the vanguard of social transformation and lead the way toward a nuclear free world. By voting down this proposal, the Academic Council reaffirmed the primary liberal values of the institution.

If the seminary as such is not a church, then the use of the analogical method to legitimate seminary endorsement of church or/and denominational public policy statements is inappropriate. If the seminary is to provide a context in which persons may freely explore a variety of interpretations of Christian ethics and public policy proposals and is to resist the temptation to become a community of politics, then it should be most restrained in adopting public policy positions.[8]

Many of its members may be in the vanguard of social transformation, for the value commitments required to sustain a liberal Christian theological school do not apply to the diverse more specialized beliefs which members of a seminary community hold. If they want to form Believers Churches whose adherents covenant to promote particular public policy proposals, they should be encouraged to do so. If they want to participate in one or more of the numerous voluntary associations in American life promoting particular public policy viewpoints, they should be encouraged to do so. The only restriction a liberal Christian theological seminary should impose is a limiting one. Members of a seminary community should make it clear that they do not speak for the seminary as such with respect either to particular public policy issues or to the specialized religious social ethic influencing their judgments on these issues.[9]

THE FUTURE

Perry LeFevre is deeply committed to the primary liberal values which have sustained this seminary during the almost half-century he has been associated with it. His commitment to fundamental liberal values is reflected in the care with which he seeks to explore contrasting interpretations of the Christian movement.

Wary of what he considers to be the excess speculation of Whitehead and Hartshorne, he has focused more sharply on the empirical side of experience. Persuaded that there is an immanental good more basic than any created good, he has sought to identify and to nurture those structures and processes in human life which evoke creative personal and social transformations to counter the evil and the banal in the world.

In light of his embodiment of the fundamental values informing the life of this liberal Christian theological seminary, it is fitting to conclude this essay with some reflections about its future. Both the fragility of the liberal idea and the relative paucity of financial resources provided by individuals and churches committed to the liberal idea raise questions about its survival beyond the first two decades of the twenty-first century.

The liberal idea is challenged by various forms of religious fundamentalism. Some, such as Islamic fundamentalism, pose no real threat to liberal Christian theological seminaries. Others, such as the so-called religious right in the United States and other forms of Christian orthodoxy, pose a minor threat; but it seems most unlikely that adherents to the modes of thought represented in that movement will impact directly on most liberal Christian seminaries.

As observed earlier, due to its widespread popularity among people in some groups historically related to liberalism, liberation theologies using the dialectic of negation and critical theory potentially pose the most serious threat to the idea of a liberal Christian theological seminary. Taken conjointly, the dialectic of negation and critical theory limit the freedom of inquiry and debate which is at the heart of a liberal seminary.

Unless people are willing to maintain a distinction between *theoria* and *praxis*, they will seek to transform the liberal Christian theological seminary into a political community committed to an orthopraxis. The embodiment of either an orthodoxy or an orthopraxis as primary institutional values would transform this liberal seminary into an indoctrination center. It would cease to be a liberal Christian theological seminary.

This liberal Christian theological seminary is a fragile entity; it needs the support of a broad company within and without an immediate seminary community to survive and to serve in the twenty-first century. It needs a student body and a faculty who, by substantial majorities, both share the fundamental liberal idea of free and open inquiry and debate about the meaning and practice of the Christian movement and also seek to develop interpretations of the Christian movement which they can maintain with intellectual and emotional integrity. It also needs the financial support of those persons within the Christian movement who share these primary liberal values and who are persuaded this particular liberal Christian theological seminary is worthy of their support.

To warrant such support, this seminary must sustain people who develop modes of thought reflecting the profundity of meaning and practice embodied within the Christian movement. Its graduates must demonstrate leadership capacities within the Christian movement and must contribute positively to the life of the broader society in which religious institutions are set.

Perry LeFevre has given full measure to foster an ethos evoking these qualities among its faculty and its graduates. It has been a privilege to be his colleague for more than thirty years. Through devotion and perspicuity he has contributed much to the self-definition of this institution and to the understanding of the meaning of a liberal Christian theological seminary. It is my hope that those who are associated with this seminary may continue the quest for scholarly and professional excellence, theological integrity, and seasonal relevance so deeply embodied in the life, thought, and work of Perry LeFevre.

ENDNOTES

1. The Chicago Theological Seminary was founded by Congregationalists in 1855. Because that denomination and its successor, the United Church of Christ, both have a congregational form of polity, its governance is different than seminaries related to denominations with Presbyterian or Episcopal polities. Its Board of Trustees is self-selected and self-perpetuating.
2. In this essay, that portion of a larger whole which impinges most directly on the development of LeFevre's thought is highlighted. Both within and without the Federated Theological Faculty, critics and those indifferent to process modes of thought were plentiful.
3. Daniel Day Williams," Theology and Truth" *The Journal of Religion* (October, 1942), Vol. XXII, No. 4, pp. 382-97, reprinted in Daniel Day Williams, *Essays in Process Theology*, edited by Perry LeFevre, (Chicago: Exploration Press, 1985) p. 30.
4. *Ibid*, pp. 33-34.
5. *Ibid.* pp. 34-35.
6. As noted earlier in the text, shorn of their Christian particularity, the fundamental values of

religious tolerance, religious pluralism, and religious liberty are also embodied in the Enlightenment and in nineteenth century English liberalism. Historically a complex interplay of Baptist, Quaker, Enlightenment, English liberal, later Congregationalist and Social Gospel ideas has contributed to the core notions which have shaped the life of this seminary for most of the twentieth century.

As noted in the body of the text, LeFevre's commitment to fundamental liberal values is reflected in the care with which he seeks to explore contrasting interpretations of the Christian movement. In his required courses in constructive theology, he sought to introduce his students to a broad and representative range of thinkers. Students were expected to develop their own constructive positions at the conclusion of their work in these courses.

7. The author was visited by a student who sought his participation in some meetings designed to develop the nuclear free proposal. The author told the student that he detested nuclear weapons, thought they were a curse on humankind, and believed their widespread use would be catastrophic for humankind. He also observed that in his judgment the mutually assured destruction strategy being pursued by the U.S. and its allies was the one most likely to prevent a nuclear holocaust. He then observed that others may disagree with his prudential judgment in this matter. In any event, he stated he was opposed on principle to any statement on the issue, pro or con, by the seminary *qua* seminary, for it should not become a community of politics.

If the seminary is to be conceived as a church, it should be understood as a catholic institution, possessing a "formless form" so protean it can encompass multiple forms of beliefs and practices within it.

8. The author says "most restrained" because he can envisage a most extraordinary situation which might require an institutional statement. Even in such a situation, members of the seminary community should seek other avenues to advance their views if at all feasible.

9. People associating with diverse interest groups and interacting with each other enrich the intellectual life of a liberal Christian theological school. Reflecting the fashionableness of the ascribed bases for social location today, the organizational bases for most of the special interest groups at this liberal seminary are gender and race. Whether this interest group configuration is adequate to evoke rich and complex intellectual interchange is moot.

Of the five special interest groups active at the Chicago Theological Seminary in the 1990-91 academic year, four were constituted primarily by gender issues and racial issues. These include a woman's concerns group, a men's concerns group, a gay and lesbian concerns group, and an African-American concerns group. The only special interest group organized on a different basis was a student chapter of the Fellowship of Reconciliation, a body with a pacifist orientation.

In addition to the FOR, the only other inclusive student groups were a Worship Committee and a Community Life Committee which are organized by the seminary to co-ordinate some inclusive events, largely for social activities or for spiritual formation.

Because special interest group and multiplication of factions ideas are deeply rooted in the American liberal tradition (e.g., *The Federalist Papers*), special interest group principles of organization are commonplace in this institution. The dialectic of negation and critical theory extant in some theological circles have played a role in creating a climate of opinion encouraging gender and race defined interest groups, but special interest group principles seem to be dominant informing notions among this seminary's participants.

CHAPTER II

To Imagine a World: Constructive Theology

by Susan Brooks Thistlethwaite

"The most important thing is vision."

Spike Lee, *Newsweek 10/2/89*

In the 1915-1916 joint Chicago Theological Seminary and University of Chicago Divinity School catalogue, the field of "Systematic Theology" has as its subheadings the divisions of "Historical Theology," "Constructive Theology" and "Practical Theology." This new term, Constructive Theology, emerged in the 1915-1916 catalogue as a way to name the kind of distinctive liberalism in theology that Widick Schroeder describes in Chapter 1. Constructive theology in these early decades of the twentieth century described an approach to theology rooted in a sense of God's continuous presence in the world, a presence best discerned through the human mind and human activity. Instead of God radically distant from the world, dropping revelation like stones onto the heads of hapless recipients, God, and hence speech about God, is found through the human condition.

The change for theological teaching should have been, and often was, dramatic. All realms of human endeavor became grist for the theological mill and all fields potential dialogue partners. The new fields of sociology, anthropology and above all, psychology could be drawn into this process.[1] James Adams, Edward Aubrey, Daniel Day Williams, all were at one time simultaneously teaching Constructive Theology in the joint program. Though, as Perry LeFevre once wryly remarked to me, their commitment to dialogue and process did not prevent each of them from teaching their particular approach to theology as the one revealed truth. But old habits die hard.

Constructive Theology developed as an approach to the tasks of theology in the twentieth century in fits and starts. Like all forms of liberalism, it was battered but ultimately not bowed by the winds of European neo-orthodoxy. The uniquely American form of European Neo-orthodoxy, "Christian Realism," is, in fact, a neo-liberalism. It is a sobered return of some liberals such as John Bennett, Robert Calhoun, H. Richard Niebuhr, Reinhold Niebuhr, and H. Shelton Smith to their social gospel roots with a deepened sense of both personal and social sin. Christian Realists, however, were not the major inheritors of the themes of Constructive Theology.

The banner of constructive theology was carried, rather, by those influenced by the empirical side of Alfred North Whitehead's thought (see Schroeder essay, p. 13) such as Henry Nelson Wieman, Bernard Loomer, Bernard Meland and Perry LeFevre and Gordon Kaufman. More recently this stream of thought has emerged in the work of Sallie McFague.

In his book describing Constructive theology as a method, Kaufman notes that the situation in which the modern theologian finds him or herself is intellectually marginal. The logical status of the central concepts with which theology deals demand radical reconception of both the task of theology and the way in which the task can be carried out. Theology can no longer conceive of itself as presenting a map of "How things are." Rather, the task of theology is like building a house or constructing a world. The best analogy to the task of theology is that of map or model.

> An analogy may be useful. Charts and models are always our constructions of a reality which is too immense, or otherwise inaccessible, to grasp without their aid. They consist of imaginative systematic orderings of selected items and elements, so brought into relation and interconnection with each other as to emphasize and thus make clearly visible to us certain features which we might otherwise overlook or not recognize at all. In some cases we can discern how closely or accurately they set forth the real structure of that which they represent; for example, with an architect's blueprints for a house the relations of chart to object are precisely definable and measurable. But in other cases this not possible at all: the relation of the models of waves and particles to those features of the actual structure of matter (or energy?) which we designate as "electrons" is impossible to specify, and the concept of electron is itself a very complex construct of the mind.[2]

In addition, there is not one mega-chart or map that will suffice for all the kinds of knowledge human beings need. For example, an accurate oil map of deposits in North Dakota will not help you drive through North Dakota; likewise, a road map will not tell you where to find oil. The task of the particular map or model is to help you get where you want to go. This is not to say that a given map does not have any correspondence to "the way things really are," but it is a particular slice of reality closely related to the concerns of the traveler. What is especially key in this way of doing theology is that the arrangement of the data is equally if not more important than the data itself. How you look at what you know is critical to understanding what it means.

CONSTRUCTIVE THEOLOGY AND LIBERATION THEOLOGY

Perry LeFevre taught Constructive Theology at CTS for just over twenty years; I have taught Constructive Theology at CTS for twelve years. Despite my training as a Systematic Theologian and my own work as a liberation and feminist theologian, I have never been motivated to change the titles of these two required courses (Constructive I and Constructive II). In fact, the textbook that I developed in the Constructive classes and edited with Mary Potter Engel is entitled, *Lift Every Voice; Constructing Christian Theologies from the Underside.* What can Liberation Theology inherit from Constructive Theology?

A key to understanding liberalism in theology is to separate liberalism as a theological method from any positions which might or might not be deemed "liberal," i.e. equal rights etc. The paradigm shift between liberalism and the older orthodoxy was that liberals saw a continuity between God and the world in contrast to the orthodox insistence on the separation of God from the world. Therefore, rather than repudiating the intellectual and social life of the broader culture, liberals (particularly in the late nineteenth and early twentieth century) embraced culture.

This whole-hearted embrace of culture was one of the roots of the neo-orthodox critique. A form of culture-Protestantism had lost the ability to critique the excesses of modern culture and to take a stand against its death-dealing proclivities. While the failure of liberals to resist pernicious political trends was clearly displayed in their failure to stand up to the Nazi regime in Germany, their uncritical attitude toward modern culture was evident long before the Nazi era in the trends leading to the First World War.

The theologies of liberation inherit both the critique of culture evident in neo-orthodoxy and the embrace of the intellectual tools of the human social sciences. To the neo-orthodox critique, the liberation theologian adds an analysis of power inequalities in society. Dominant culture is to be critiqued for this exploitation of the poor and marginalized; the experience of the marginalized, however, is the location of God's revelation in history. Hence, where modern liberals used psychology to understand the human mind, liberation theologians use economic analysis not merely to understand the world, but to change it (to cite Marx).

Liberation theologians embrace the turn to culture that liberals began. But for the liberation theologian, social location is critical. The turn to social location is called CONTEXTUALITY, a common theme among the many different liberation theologies around the world. The liberals, particularly of the social gospel stripe, opened the door to the social location emphasis of liberation theology in America. Keep in mind that one of the most prominent North American liberals, H. R. Niebuhr (who became a trenchant critic of liberalism), wrote *The Social Sources of Denominationalism.* In this classic work, Niebuhr cautions

> Yet an exclusively religious interpretation [of denominationalism] especially a doctrinal one, is likely to miss the point of the whole development even more completely than does an exclusively economic explanation. For if religion supplies the energy, the goal, and the motive of sectarian movements, social factors no less decidedly supply the occasion, and determine the form the religious dynamic will take.[3]

Niebuhr's proposal that the theologian doing ecclesiology take substantive account of the perspective of the class and race constituency of the particular North American Protestant (white) denominations is a classic text for theology done from the analysis of social location.

Interestingly, the early liberation theologians were for the large part Latin American Catholic males, often clerics, who protested the cultural captivity of their church to the totalitarian political regimes of Central and Latin America. Their theological protest has emphasized the development of the notions of human agency, freedom and history, themes quite resonant with those of Euro-Atlantic Protestantism.

African American male theologians and Latin American theologians have continued the emphasis on human sin of the neo-orthodox critique, but they have brought to this critique a notion of evil as structural and systemic. Womanist theologians (African American women who use a race, class and gender analysis) and Mujerista theologians (Hispanic women who use a race/ethnicity, class and gender analysis) employ both an emphasis on systemic evil and the resources of the community for change.

Native Americans and white North American feminists have concentrated more on constructing a new view of nature, a theme largely neglected in the liberal emphasis on political analysis. Native American, white feminists, Womanists, Mujerista, and Minjung theologians, both male and female, tend to use story, folktale, song and poetry as part of their theological method.

A contextual emphasis largely ignored for a long time by many of the above has been the critique of heterosexism, the view that two genders, male and female, are the only norm for human sexual existence. Lesbians and gay men, particularly in several racial and ethnic communities in the United States, have begun to explore this context. Human sexuality has all but been ignored by theologians throughout Christian history as a realm for constructive thinking about human life and work. The influx of those oppressed because of gender or gender orientation into theology has opened the door to this contextual work.

Constructive theology is an excellent vehicle for allowing these various voices in theology to emerge in distinctive ways. Where the Marxists urge us all not to merely understand the world but to change it, Constructive theologians underline that sometimes one has to imagine the world can be different in order to struggle against those forces who would have us believe that this order is unchangeable. Marcuse has said, "The success of the system is to make alternatives unthinkable."

The quotation from Spike Lee with which I began this chapter is particularly apt. As Perry LeFevre noted in his remarks at his retirement dinner, Chicago Theological Seminary has a markedly new constituency.

> I remember Archie Hargraves joining us as the first full time African American faculty member and sharing in the beginning of the Center for Black Religious Studies.
>
> And in all of this there emerged the conviction that the Seminary had a special calling to be responsive to the needs of the churches on the southside. And little by little with the coming of other African American faculty and two Presidents the color of the student body began to change.
>
> Part of this change came through the increasing number of S. African students, following Ross and Martha Snyder's work in S. Africa in the early 1960's. And then others came from other parts of Africa and from many other parts of the world. Who can forget the impact of people like Bonga Goba or Jim Cochrane or any number of others, both black and white who came to us a part of this stream.
>
> And the women came in increasing numbers, and Rabbis came and more and more second career persons came, enlarging the age spectrum of our community. And the Asians came. And gays and lesbians came as it was clear that race, gender, nationality, sexual orientation and age were no barriers to theological education at CTS.[4]

As Perry LeFevre so aptly describes, the number of African American women and men, white women, and men (and now a very few women) from around the world have increased at CTS to the point where 'globalization' is not a catch-word, but a simple empirical description of the students and increasingly, the faculty.

The theological work that these students need to do is to define their own context both in an individual and social sense and then to work out a way of addressing their context in a way that mines both the theological traditions of Christianity and the resources of their individual communities. Global village is another catch-word that becomes empirically apt at CTS. These contexts interrelate. Here students must learn to do theology that is accountable to the other contexts and to the power differences among them.

A CRITIQUE OF CONSTRUCTIVE THEOLOGY

Liberation theology, contextual theology, minjung theology, mujerista theology, African American theology: these theological perspectives may find connections to the way Constructive Theology has been done at Chicago Theological Seminary. Yet, this essay would not be an accurate description of the changes that are taking place in Constructive Theology unless some of the tensions are named as well.

The work of one of the most famous constructive theologians, Gordon Kaufman (whose essay on Constructive Theology I cited earlier) illustrates both the yes and the no that theology done from the margins of history has to say to constructive. As noted above, Kaufman's proposal is that constructive theology is a project of the human imagination in reconceiving the relation of

God, world and human beings. One of the central tasks of constructive theology is to make a meaningful world and one of the ways to accomplish that task is to excite the human imagination to find a place in that world.

Kaufman's Presidential address to the American Academy of Religion "Theology for a Nuclear Age," became a widely read book of the same name. In this book, Kaufman takes a constructive theological approach to the problem of God in the nuclear age and notes that "God conceived in terms of the metaphor of creativity or constructive power. . . will be of a very different sort from a God conceived in terms of violent destructiveness."[5]

Kaufman's enterprise illustrates very well the genius of Protestant liberalism out of which Constructive theology has emerged: its embrace of the immanence of God in the world. This is, of course, the point most often cited by critics of liberalism as its weakness; that is, that its doctrine of God is too subjective, that revelation becomes synonymous with human experience, and hence that there is no judgment on evil.

Liberalism has faults certainly, but the presence of God in the world is not one of them. Its weakness is rather at the level of theological anthropology. Liberalism buys fully into the myth of the individual as the locus of an independently functioning objective reason. The true weakness of liberalism is not immanence, but rather a half-hearted immanence that is colored by romanticism and confined to a particular class and race experience. The whole human being including the human body and society is never fully embraced, and hence a mind-body dualism remains in its commitment to immanence.

When I say that anthropology is the problem, I mean that the solitary, reflecting individual finds him or herself essentially alone. It is well to remember that the "God above God" of Paul Tillich (on whom Gordon Kaufman, Sallie McFague and other constructive theologians draw heavily) is Tillich's answer to his assessment of the fundamental human existential dilemma—estrangement.[6]

And so Kaufman writes, "as we mature to adulthood, we become aware that no human being can be absolutely relied on."[7] In a similar vein, while Sallie McFague claims to have learned from the women's movement, her *Models of God* does not mention the importance of economic arrangements in our understanding of God, nor does she emphasize human solidarity at all.

In sum, while the major constructive theologians of the twentieth century have contributed to bringing God closer to the world, they have been less successful in the effort to bring human beings closer together. In short, while they have objected to God's otherness and located the beginning point for theological reflection in the human mind, they do not have a companion anthropology strong enough to support their proposals for world reconstruction via imagination.

A COMMUNITY FOR THEOLOGICAL WORK

Rare is the constructive theologian, therefore, who recognizes that the companion of God's immanence is the community of human beings with whom God exercises immance. It was, therefore, a joy to me to hear Perry LeFevre describe the need for such community in his address.

> For me, experiencing the changing shape and color of our community has been a great joy. The Seminary has come to embody, in faculty, students and administration, the inclusiveness that Christian community is meant to express. It is both a challenge and a marvelously enriching reality for all of us. Sometimes we have trouble with the language, not just the words, but the cross cultural communication that is required; sometimes we have trouble transcending the particularity of the intensified consciousness of the diverse groups. Here too we need to make the transformation of consciousness which Erickson writes about from I to WE.[8]

The enduring contribution of constructive is the insistence on the capacity of the human imagination to conceive the possibility of community where there is only fragmentation, to imagine there might be justice where injustice is the norm, to claim that there could be such a thing as peace when the newspaper blandly records a kind of Hobbesian war of all against all. Because we cannot struggle towards something that we cannot envisage.

The distinctive contribution of the theologies of liberation to the journey of community about which Perry speaks is that the transcendence is not despite differences of gender, race, class, sexual orientation or nationality, but through a recognition of these differences and a commitment in community to struggle against the stratifications in power and privilege along these lines.

In the Introduction to the *Lift Every Voice* volume I wrote,

> Lastly, a word of caution. This book will not tell you much if you enter it as a tourist. Learning the method of the theologies of liberation, understanding the commitment to do theology contextually, communally, and concretely means asking yourself, "in my social location, where is justice struggling to be born and how can I help?" As Audre Lorde has written, "Survival is not an academic skill."[9]

This is true of learning in the constructive theology courses at Chicago Theological Seminary. You cannot be a tourist. Theology emerges out of the commitment to be in community, to struggle against the forces ranged against the well-being of humanity and to imagine together that there might be a different way. These aren't easy courses to teach, and the students tell me they are not easy courses to take, but I think I could get some consensus on the fact that they have been fun.

NOTES AND REFERENCES

1. The term "process" here is used non-technically to describe the bridges this approach to theology tried to build with the broader culture.
2. Gordon D. Kaufman, *An Essay on Theological Method* (Missoula, Montana: Scholars Press, 1975), p. 27.
3. H. Richard Niebuhr, *The Social Sources of Denominationalism* (New York: Henry Holt and Co., 1929), p. 27.
4. Perry LeFevre, "On Reminiscing," in *The Chicago Theological Seminary Register* (Spring 1992) Vol. LXXXII, No. 2, p. 19.
5. Gordon Kaufman, *Theology for a Nuclear Age* (Philadelphia: Westminster, 1985), pp. 25-26.
6. Paul Tillich, *The Courage to Be* (New Haven: Yale University Press, 1952), pp. 48, 52, 54, 75-77, 87, 90, 125-7, 132, 138, 169.
7. Gordon Kaufman, *The Theological Imagination* (Philadelphia: Westminster, 1981), p. 60.
8. Perry LeFevre, Ibid, p. 21.
9. Susan Thistlethwaite and Mary Potter Engel, *Lift Every Voice: Constructing Christian Theology from the Underside* San Francisco: Harper and Row, 1990), p. 14, quoting Audre Lorde, "The Master's Tools Will Never Dismantle the Master's House," in *This Bridge Called My Back*, ed. Cherie Moraga and Gloria Anzaldua (Watertown, MA: Persephone, 1981), p. 100.

CHAPTER III

Theological Anthropology

by Theodore W. Jennings

One of the characteristic themes of the writing and teaching of Perry Lefevre has been theological anthropology, that is, an attempt to understand humanity in the light of the insights of the Christian tradition[1]. In this essay I wish to focus upon the question of the possibility of such an enterprise under the conditions of what may be called "post-modernity."

THE POST-MODERN PROBLEM

Perhaps the most provocative thesis of Michel Foucault is that the new era into which we are entering is characterized by the disappearance of "man" as the self-evident starting point and the certain foundation for reflection[2]. This thesis is widely identified as one of the characteristic features of post-modernity. But if the human is displaced from the center and ground of thought, the position the human has held in modernity, then what does this mean for the role and place of a theological anthropology in the post modern situation?

In order to see what is a stake here we may recall that the modern period in European thought was characterized by what Kant called his second Copernican revolution. The original Copernican revolution, of course, had displaced the earth from its position at the center of the universe, introducing first a helio-centric view of the world and subsequently a de-centered view, a cosmos in which or for which there was no center at all.

The Kantian revolution may be viewed as a re-centering of thought in the subject. If the world "out there" could no longer supply the stable point of reference then this would be supplied by the knowing, willing, judging subject. Now this philosophical-epistemological move does not occur in a vacuum. It takes place within a European culture of enlightenment that reflected and amplified this "anthropocentrism." Corresponding to this philosophical move are a variety of parallel developments in economics, politics, the arts and religion. Thus the political sphere moves toward the discourse of the "rights of man". In art we witness the emergence of the human visage in painting and the emergence of the novel as the characteristic literary form supplemented by drama in which character takes the stage in order to disclose a coherent interiority. In religion we see the emergence of pietism and evangelical fervor as characteristic expressions. All of this is set within the political economy of middle class capitalism with its ideology of the rugged individual. This period of modernity proved fruitful in many ways, not least in the emergence of the so-called human sciences.

Theology was able to make common cause with modernity by placing the emphasis upon humanity as the proper subject of inquiry concerning the divine activity. Thus Schleiermacher could place at the center of his reflection the "god-consciousness" of the person, and Kierkiegaard could place the human dilemma of grasping the infinite within the conditions of the finite as the heart of reflection. The first half of this century saw the triumph of this idea in the emergence of personalism in the United States, then of existentialism in Europe, and in the neo-Schleiermachian emphasis upon ultimate concern and the absolute awareness of the unconditioned in Tillich and the emergence of psychology, especially depth psychology, as the preferred dialogue partner of a theological anthropology.

In many ways then the question of anthropology-the proper understanding of humanity-came to be self-evidently the starting point, center and goal of intellectual reflection in philosophy, the human sciences and theology.

However the self-evidence of this subject is now called into question. This occurs of course in the realm of intellectual culture with the announcement of the end of the "age of man" . But it is not only in high intellectual culture that this occurs. We may see it also in the emergence of the "new novel" in which the old categories of plot and character take a back seat to episode and monologue. In painting, the human figure as well as the world disappear in favor of form and color in the various schools of abstract and cubist painting. In sculpture the experimentation with line and form and frozen motion replace representation of the human and the human world. Similar transformations occur in all the arts. In political economy the activity of the entrepreneur is elbowed off the stage in favor of market forces and regulation and the sphere of politics becomes increasingly irrelevant, a kind of side show to the burocratization of the public sphere.

The point of this is not to lament the passing of a previous era, but simply to note that a sea-change is in process in culture and society. It would be folly to lament this change. After all the era of "enlightenment humanism" is the era of colonialism, of slavery and racism, of the economic savagery of raw capitalism and so on. In many ways the benign face of modern humanism has served to disguise the virulent barbarity of modern culture and society.

One of the ways in which the ambiguity of modernity comes to expression has to do with the way in which the corner stone of modernity, the idea of "man" served as an imperial or hegemonic imposition of the part for the whole. We are increasingly aware that much that previously passed for reflection on the nature of the human was in fact characterized by partial and ideological substitutes for humanity as such. Thus much reflection that claimed a certain universality simply ignored or wrote off the experience of women, of those who were excluded from the locations of power and privilege, of those who were not within the Euro-American center. Thus what passed itself off as a view of humanity was often no more than the reflection of a particular group or party. And the "knowledge" thus acquired was used to invalidate the experience and thus the "humanity" of those whose position was eccentric to the system of representation that had acquired hegemony.

But in our time these repressed humanities have begun to find their voice with results that are disconcerting for the tradition of "humanism". When women, for example, protest against a androcentric view of humanity, the result is a breaking apart of the human subject. In so far as humanity was constituted androcentrically then the human subject proposed by feminism appears as an other humanity. Something similar occurs when other repressed humanities appear: that of indigenous peoples, of the underclass, of marginalized peoples generally. Instead of a unitary subject known as "man" we seem to encounter a bewildering variety of humanities. The stable subject of modernity becomes a complex and disparate plurality. And the guardians of the humanistic tradition often respond in such a way as to indicate that this plural subject is indeed a threat to their basic world view.

The contemporary scene, then, appears to be characterized by the marginalization of the person from cultural, political and economic reality and the fracturing of the unity of the human subject into a plurality of competing humanities. Thus the human subject can no longer serve as the center and given of reflection. What are we to make of the possibility of a theological anthropology when the self-evidence of this starting point and center of reflection has come into question?

In should be noted that it is no solution to our difficulty simply to transfer our attention to some other theme within the compass of theological reflection. For in respect of the introduction of an apparently irreducible plurality in interpretation, no theme is immune. Thus the plurality of standpoints results in the fracturing of consensus with respect to doctrines of God and Christ, as well as sin and salvation.   Simply changing the subject then will not help us. Nor does this seem possible for theology in any case since anthropology is an unavoidable theme for theological reflection. In order to clarify this point I turn first to a consideration of the way in which the question of the character of humanity as such comes into play within the Christian tradition.

THE QUESTION OF HUMANITY

That humanity as such should be the subject of theological thematization is not self evident from the standpoint of the phenomenology of religion. We should recall that religious ideology is often concerned primarily with the character of the adherents of the tribal or religious grouping, with the insiders of the religious system and not with the outsiders who can be relegated to a decidedly secondary role.

Even in the religious framework of the hellenistic world with the inclusion of social groups from a number of distinct tribal, national and religious identities the notion of humanity as such was by no means self-evident. For example, the inherent elitism of gnostic anthropology assured that only a certain group would be in any true sense fully human: those who were either by nature gnostic, or those who were educable. The vast majority of persons would be excluded. Similarly the class structure of the city states assured that reflections on the human as citizen would exclude in principle women and slaves from consideration. Where the conception of humanity as such could come to the fore as in stoicism, this was made possible by the notion of the dispersion of the seed of the logos and so of rationality throughout humanity.

Christianity, like stoicism, was committed to the idea of humanity as such. This owed in part at least to the identity of Christianity as a movement that was extended in principle to all persons. We will return to this shortly but here I want to focus attention on the way in which humanity as such is thematized in Paul, the earliest documentary evidence we have for Christian reflection.

Two passages from Paul are especially important in suggesting how the theme of humanity is thematized for Christian theology.

> Thus it is written:"The first human Adam, became a living being"; the last Adam became a life-giving spirit....The first human was from the earth, a human of dust: the second human is from heaven. As was the human of dust, so are those who are of the dust; and as is the human of heaven, so are those who are of heaven. Just as we have borne the image of the human of dust, we shall also bear the image of the human of heaven... I Corinthians 15:45, 47-49

> Then as one human's trespass led to condemnation for all humanity, so one human's act of justice leads to acquittal and life for all humanity. Romans 5:18

In these and related passages we find humanity as the object of creation, as the subject of sin and as the object of redemption.

For our purposes what is important is that the "drama of salvation" concerns the whole of humanity. It is not something that concerns some persons or groups of persons but rather is from the very beginning concerned with humanity as such. Indeed it appears that Christian theology cannot exist without this orientation to humanity.

It should be noted that the notion of original or "natural" sin whatever its inconveniences does have the advantage of eliminating the possibility of the division in principle of the human race into the righteous and the sinners. The notion of original sin "democratizes" the idea of sin making it universal in character.

In this connection we may note that the view of Adam and Eve as the common ancestors of humanity served a similar function. Today "fundamentalists " focus upon this as a test of the view of biblical inerrancy and have lost sight altogether of its regulatory function. As Anselm makes clear the notion of Adam and Eve as common ancestors is what gives to humanity its racial unity, what Marx termed its "species" character. Indeed for Anselm what makes the salvation of fallen humanity possible but the salvation of fallen angels impossible is that humans have a common ancestry and so are of a single species while angels lack this formal solidarity and so cannot be the subject of atonement.[3] Atonement for Anselm thus takes the form of the assumption of the species reality of humanity by the divine in such a way as to constitute a personal unity which then is capable of rendering "satisfaction" to the divine honor for its sin.

In general the unity of the human species is what makes the talk of salvation possible for patristic authors as well. The divine Word that had created humanity becomes one with humanity as such in the incarnation, resulting in the in-hominization of the divine Word (Athanasius). Hence also Irenaeus' view that Christ lived to be 50 in order to recapitulate the life-stages of humanity in general.

It is thus clear from this cursory review of some of the basic theological themes that Christian theology cannot evade the question of the nature and destiny of humanity.

THE DISPLACEMENT OF HUMANITY

If humanity remains an indispensable theme for theological reflection, are we then unable to respond positively to the transformation from a modern to a post-modern treatment of this theme? Must theology engage in a rear-guard opposition to these developments in culture and society? I will suggest three ways in which theology can make the post-modern problematic its own in relation to theological anthropology.

One of the characteristics of the post-modern problematic has been the displacement of the person in favor of the recognition that other forces and structures have taken center stage. This marginalization of the human subject may in fact have an important corollary in the theological tradition. For one theme sounded clearly in theological anthropology from Paul to Luther has been the secondary and derivative character of human reality in relation to external forces and structures.

Thus the human condition apart from grace has been understood to be fundamentally determined by captivity to "principalities and powers" that enslave humanity to the "law of sin and death". There is a certain isomorphism here with the post-modern intuition that humanity is in fact governed by external realities. The autonomous sensibility, consciousness and will of the modern subject has been exposed as an epiphenomenon of a socially constructed unconscious (Freud's theory of repression) and an economically determined class interest (Marx).

On the other hand Pauline anthropology proposes the transformation of this enslaved subject by way of the intervention of an alien power (grace) which summons humanity into a new reality. Even here the human is determined by an external though now not heteronomous force of which the new humanity is an effect rather than self-sufficient cause.

Moreover the human is understood within this tradition of theological anthropology as a "site of struggle" in which the forces of sin and grace, of flesh and spirit contend vigorously for supremacy.

Now to be sure these insights are expressed in the tradition in ways that appropriate the symbolics of myth. In this sense these perspectives are decidedly "pre-modern". At the same time these mythologically derived symbolic structures offer to contemporary theological reflection ways to appropriate the post-modern awareness that humanity is not to be conceived as the master of its own destiny but as co-determined by forces that struggle for ascendancy within the sphere of the human. In this way the project of demystification of the illusion of a fully autonomous subjectivity and of an innocent personalism— the project, that is, of a hermeneutics of suspicion directed at the modern construction of the human subject— finds an important point of contact in the religious and theological tradition.

THE DIVERSITY OF HUMANITY

We have seen that one of the features of the post-modern problematic of anthropology is the recognition that the human, so far from being a unitary subject, is actually composed of competing and apparently irreconcilable distinctions. There are a plurality of "humanities" that the modern construction of the human subject did not take into account and indeed seems to have repressed from awareness. How can theology respond to this altered circumstance?

The unity of humanity entailed in the symbol of common ancestry (Adam) and common destiny (Christ), while it eliminates the possibility of discrimination between the more and less human or the disqualification of some from humanity nevertheless does not entail that this humanity is simply a uniform given.

The theological orientation to humanity as such as the object of the good news does not seem to entail that some or other given form of humanity is the norm or standard in terms of which the humanity of the "other" is to be denied. Rather it seems to mean that the typical ways of dividing persons into opposing categories are suspended, at least as regards all that is fundamental to the faith. Thus Paul can speak of the abrogation of the divisions that in other contexts had been regarded as fundamental. That in Christ there is neither Jew nor Gentile means that religious categorization is abolished. That is, humanity must be conceived as inclusive of significantly different religious perspectives. No religion has a monopoly on humanity. Similarly that there is neither Greek nor barbarian entails the abolition of cultural privilege. This means that humanity may not be defined from the point of view of one set of cultural assumptions to which all other cultures must adhere in order to be included among humanity. That in Christ there is neither slave nor free would indicate that the attempt to define humanity in terms of the class privilege of the masters is undermined. Perhaps the most radical of these assertions, and the one whose implications have been least attended to in the official theological tradition, is that in Christ there is neither male nor female. This entails that the male privilege of defining humanity on its own terms is fundamentally undercut. In all of these ways the orientation to humanity as old and new Adam is no merely harmless liberalism but actually undercuts the divisions by which humanity is differentially distributed and valued.

Nor is this limited to the Pauline tradition. It has important antecedents in the Jesus tradition as well. Certainly the synoptic symbol of the "son of man" may be understood as a corporate reality whose initial but by no means exclusive bearer is Jesus.[4] The new humanity that is lord of the sabbath, that has power to forgive sins and that must suffer persecution is by no means restricted to Jesus but rather includes those who follow in his way. Thus Jesus' mission calls persons into this new humanity in which hegemonic and hierarchical structures and divisions based on race, sex, class, and religious privilege are abolished.

In this sense it is clear that it is inappropriate to look back to the period of enlightenment humanism as the period of the human. Instead it becomes clear that the humanity then spoken of was a truncated and fragmentary humanity, a premature foreclosure of the human. What has been lost is the unquestioned hegemony of the Euro-American middle class male as the defining representative of humanity. The clarification of the fragmentary character of this reality and the exposure of its imposture does not mean the end of a theological anthropology but rather is one of the conditions for further reflection on humanity as a specifically theological theme.

THE ESCHATOLOGICAL HUMAN

We have seen that a response to the post-modern situation may entail a recuperation of an understanding of humanity as composed of a plurality of humanities. In what sense then is the unity "in Christ" of this diversity of humanities to be understood. The difficulty is to identify this unity without denying the plurality.

One of the most promising ways to achieve this end is by means of the eschatological structure of the Christian mythos. Within this framework humanity is not a given received from a fixed past but is rather an object of hope.   The human does not (yet) exist. Rather the human is that which is yet to be actualized. This is consonant with the view that humanity is not the center or basis of reflection but is rather determined by forces or structures outside itself. Similarly this coheres with the view that no existing form of humanity is licensed to serve as the defining type of humanity as such. On an eschatological view then the diversity of humanities is unified not in one of its already existing forms but rather in that which is hoped for: a humanity beyond the polarization of class, culture, race and gender. Each of these humanities makes an irreplaceable contribution to the realization of this unification of humanity. From a theological point of view then the "truly human" appears proleptically in the new Adam as Jesus Christ but is still "under construction" in the mission and ministry of this Christ.

This new humanity is therefore by no means simply an empirical reality. Rather "it does not yet appear what we shall be". [I John 3:2] That is, this new humanity is under construction. It begins to emerge only as egoism is abolished in favor of a style of generous and indeed sacrificial love and commitment to the actualization of this reality.

This eschatological horizon enables us to bring to expression some of the basic themes of a theological anthropology within the context of the post-modern situation.

CONCLUSION

The transition from a modern to a post-modern context of theological reflection does not mean the end of a specifically theological anthropology. As we have seen the question of a theological anthropology is deeply embedded in the Christian mythos. It cannot be eradicated from the reflection that seeks to clarify and apply that mythos.

Nor does this transition mean that theological anthropology is placed in an untenable position. As we have seen, the post-modern context allows certain important features of theological anthropology to come more clearly into focus than seemed possible in the period of "modernity". Growing awareness of the way in which external forces govern subjectivity, and of the ideological mystification involved in the imposition of a fragment of humanity as the image of humanity as such open up a reappraisal of forgotten theological insights.

But the transition from modernity to post-modernity does not mean that all of the concerns and insights of modernity are simply to be left behind at the portal to this brave new world. Essential features of modernity continue to find expression. Among these the intention of developing an interpretation of the faith that does not rely upon an appeal to heteronomous authority but rather is open to unrestricted investigation and to procedures of verification/falsification in the public arena is an abiding characteristic of the reflection called for in our time. Moreover the commitment to seek the best insights of human sciences and of critical thought remains untrammeled. Finally a commitment to the liberation of humanity from dehumanizing forces and imprisoning structures even when these are legitimated by religious or quasi-religious appeal continues to characterize the project of a post-modern, as it did a modern, theological anthropology.

Notes and References

1. Perry LeFevre *Understandings of Man* (Philadelphia, Westminster Press, 1966) and *Man: Six Modern Interpretations* (Philadelphia, Geneva Press, 1968).
2. Michel Foucault *The Archeology of Knowledge and the Discourse on Language* (ET New York, Pantheon, 1972) pp. 1-17Ø.
3. Anselm *Cur Deus Homo* Book II chapter xxi
4. See my essay "The Martyrdom of the Son of Man" in *Text and Logos: The Humanistic Interpretation of the New Testament* (Atlanta, Scholars Press, 1990) pages 229-246.

CHAPTER IV

Left-Handed Prayer

by Dow Edgerton

"Lessing has said that, if God held all truth in [the] right hand, and in [the] left hand held the lifelong pursuit of it, [God] would choose the left hand."[1]

"In the fundamental insecurity of all of our lives, each of us faces the question of trust. What can one finally trust? It is the question which gives all human life a religious dimension, for the question of final trust is the question of God. Is there anything which will not betray?"[2]

The question at the foundation of human life is the question of trust, Perry LeFevre has written. In the face of the forked, crossed, torn, and contradictory world of human experience the question of existence is "What can we trust?" It is the ultimate question, which is to say, the religious question. When we speak of a search for truth, or mystery, or power, or freedom, all of these may be understood as different dimensions and dynamics of this search for what is trustworthy. When we speak of salvation, it is of this same search that we speak: "Is there anything that makes it possible for us as men and women to live with a sense of meaning and fulfillment in the face of ambiguity, tragedy, and oppression? Only such a reality could be trusted unconditionally."[3]

The search for what can be trusted is the work of a lifetime. It is the work of the whole life of the whole person, thinking, feeling, loving, working, playing, struggling, resting. It is the work of each day, and each day testifies in the most immediate way to what it is a person trusts. The question of trust, therefore, is not at the periphery but at the center; it is not the question provoked only or chiefly through encounters with the extraordinary, but in and through the most ordinary moments of a life, of a single day. The story of a life is the story of this search, undertaken in the landscape at hand, in the company of whoever they may be whose faces confront us, whose voices we hear.

If trust is the religious question, Perry LeFevre has taught, then prayer is the religious act. "The primal religious act is prayer. It is the reaching out of the whole being in search or in affirmation."[4] This reaching is what makes words and acts into prayer. It is the search for and affirmation of what is trustworthy, the truth which may be trusted with one's life, and which may only be known through such trust.

Trust is, indeed, a way of knowing. We know truth one way when we think about it, describe it, argue it. We know truth in a different way when we trust ourselves to it, and know the truth which can only unfold through all the days of a life. This is, I believe, the proper meaning of the word "faith". This is also, I believe, what it means to choose the left hand.

We may use this insight about prayer to understand what is at stake both in the prayer of the church together and the prayer of the people alone. Held in the left hand the patterns of public prayer become liturgical forms for seeking such trustworthy truth. Petition, intercecession, praise, thanksgiving, confession, all become ways of telling a different dimension of the search. Each names a distinct aspect of human experience and in the face of what is named calls for or celebrates the coming of truth which will not betray us.

In the left hand, petition searches to tell the truth of our need. It is the language of absence, longing, the call for God rising up. In petition prayer names the disappointment and betrayal of the people by what they have trusted. In petition prayer struggles to tell the truth of our ownmost lack and cries out for healing, justice, comfort, mercy, bread.

In the left hand, intercession is telling the truth of the stranger's need, the neighbor's, the enemy's. It joins the cry of other voices to call on their behalf, and sometimes may even give voice to what has remained silent or been silenced. It calls for a common justice, mercy, peace; it arises from the same wells of compassion and imagination as vision does, and prophecy, and tears. Intercession calls for the holy city to come, and soon.

In the left hand, confession struggles to tell the truth of our sin. It names aloud the power of death at work through us, our captivity to it, and our inability to free ourselves. Far from being a language of self-accusation and fear, it is a language of recognition, and release - for it is encompassed by the truth of mercy and forgiveness. Confession of sin, therefore, is also a confession of trust in the power of God to cleanse, heal, and set free.

In the left hand, thanksgiving is a way of telling the truth about the "giftedness" of our lives. It undercuts in a most profound way the myths of self-sufficiency and independence, through naming the gifts by which we live and confessing the name of the giver. Thanksgiving celebrates the particular experiences through which the people have recognized their trust validated and their distrust overcome.

Finally, in the left hand praise is a way of telling the truth by affirming the presence of God. Praise is response to that presence, a presence which is most powerfully met as an experience of freedom in the present which anticipates the fulfillment of freedom in the future. Praise, we could say, is the eruption of freedom into speech, especially if we understand speech to go beyond its usual sense to include the fullest expression of which we are capable. The experience we describe from one side as freedom, however, is "freedom-in-the-presence" or "because-of-the-presence" of what is ultimately trustworthy. It is the presence of God, the church testifies, which brings freedom.

So each of the forms of public prayer, when held in the left hand, may be understood as expressions of the great search and affirmation which are foundational to human life. By understanding each of them in this way, in fact, we can understand better how they need, support, and shape one another. It can also be seen, however, how empty and sterile public prayer becomes when it loses connection to so vital a human struggle. Perhaps we could call that "right-handed prayer" because it holds on to truth as a possession to own rather than a life to live, it holds on to truth which does not need the lives of the people to come to expression. When the writer of II Timothy laments over those who have the form of religion but deny the power, it is a lament over this very loss.

Through public prayer, Ted Jennings has argued, the church teaches prayer. It models in an essentialized way a life of prayer. This is more than the teaching of prayers. Prayer as words and rites are secondary, of course - far secondary - to what lies at the heart of prayer. What is vital is to discern the heart which *makes* prayer prayer, and makes prayer of whatever else has this heart. The reaching out of the whole being is what makes prayer, and makes it of whatever the acts are through which one reaches. "At the heart of real prayer is passion, intensity, trust," and where this heart is found, whatever the form, there is prayer.[5]

Thus every action through which the human heart is centered in the concern for what is ultimately trustworthy is prayer.[6] The liturgy at the communion table is no more prayer than that of the kitchen table. The liturgy of confession is no more prayer than asking forgiveness of the person you have wronged. Far from being a devaluing of liturgy, this is the strongest affirmation of it. If there is a goal to Christian liturgy, then it is surely this: to teach us to live. If there is a fulfillment of Christian liturgy, then it is surely this: the transformation of life into search and affirmation, into testimony, into prayer.

To pray with the left hand, then, is to live an ordinary day in the search for the trustworthy truth. Left-handed prayer is a search for truth. It is a search through which the human spirit seeks to tell the truth and hear it, to embrace truth and to be embraced, to know and be known.

> "And because prayer is a form of love and care and the concern for justice it must inevitably involve pain and suffering as we see and feel empathically the suffering and injustice which are everywhere present and as we extend ourselves in acts of care, compassion and justice. There is the mark of the cross on the truly human life, even as there was on Jesus' life and ministry."[7]

So left-handed prayer is made of the forked, crossed, torn, and contradictory reality of a day. It is an attempt to see, hear, feel, think, act, seek, and praise *in*, *through*, and *with* the terms of the day at hand. Rather than an escape, it seeks to find and trust, to be faithful, here and now.

"What are the ordinary means of grace?" the catechism asks. A remarkable question: "ordinary" and "grace" together! Isn't grace precisely what is extraordinary? free? uncontained? bestowed purely by the good pleasure of the good

God? And yet the question, however unintentionally, testifies more than it knows. There are, indeed, ordinary means, and they are even more ordinary than a person might imagine. This is the work of left-handed prayer: to recognize how deeply an ordinary day is marked, how ordinary the means of extraordinary grace are.

In one of Gerard Manley Hopkins poems, "In Memory of Alphonsus Rodriguez, Laybrother of the Society of Jesus," the poet contrasts the life of outward exploit and heroism, seen and celebrated by others, with a different kind of struggle:

> But be the war within, the heroic breast not outward steeled,
> Earth hears no hurtle then, from fiercest fray.
> Yet God (that hews mountains, continents, earth all out,
> Veins violets, and tall trees makes more and more)
> Could crowd career with conquest while there went
> Those years and years by of world without event
> That in Majorca, Alphonso watched the door.[8]

The poem evokes so powerfully the immediacy and sacramentality of the moments of an ordinary day. To live an ordinary day... But what could be harder to do? Who can claim to have done so much? A pilgrimage may be easier than a day! A great quest may be easier than a single day! Some task which is dangerous, demanding, and full of the bright din of conflict may be easier than the ordinary day.

And for some even prayer itself, to pray at all, may be the most difficult of tasks. For some the first prayer may be "teach me to pray," and we may find that this is itself the work of a lifetime. Learning to listen, to see, to feel, to speak, to tell the truth, to sing the truth, to trust the truth, these simplest foundations and gates of prayer may be for some the most difficult of mountains. That is no excuse from the task, of course, for as Perry LeFevre has written (following Paul), "When we do not know how or what to pray, this too, should be part of our prayer. In our very acknowledgement of our condition the Spirit prays in us and through us."[9]

It is among such people as these that I count myself, those for whom the first prayer is a lifetime's work. If that has a melodramatic sound then let me say it more modestly: it is more than enough work for a day, and I do not claim to have held much at all in either left hand or right.

Yet because I wish to honor and celebrate my colleague, mentor, and friend, I want to do more than to write about what he has written. I want to take it to myself and take up the task for myself: to turn to the work of listening, seeing, feeling, speaking, singing, and trusting. What you'll find here, then, are the attempts during a period of days, and at different moments of a day, to learn to pray. I do not claim them to be poems, nor to be public prayer, certainly. I make no claim about *them* at all, in fact, only a claim about what I have tried to do. My mentor, colleague, and friend has taught me in many ways about the importance of an honesty of spirit. I offer back, therefore, with respect and love, what I have been able to do with some of the days and life at hand.

I.

Teach me to pray, I pray.

After the spell of the night,
After the untellable journey and return
After those mercies of breath and blood
Which have kept me once again,

Before any word has been spoken,
Before I have taken up my name
Before I have seen my face in the mirror,
Before this hand closes upon the day.

Now, while the still light fills the window,
Now, while the air moves the curtain,
Now, while anything could be said,
Now, while anything could be heard,

Teach me to listen, I pray.
Teach me to speak, I pray.
Teach me to pray, I pray.

II.

There is nothing strange in the sickness of this friend,
Nothing strange in the possibility of her death.
It is, after all, what comes to every person.
I have seen it in my own eyes sometimes, looking back
In unexpected reflections before I could compose my face,
And I know, too, that any time at all is purest gift.
Hearing the news was not strange, either,
In the familiar voice moments ago.
What are voices for, if not this telling of the truth
Which has made us friends? What is friendship for,
If not such listening which makes your heart hollow
And loud with echoes, loud with sadness and love?
And what is a heart for, if not this?

What is strange is the lisping sound of the page turning, now,
And the bending sound the paper makes,
Like thin metal flexing in a low and brittle thunder.
The sound of the printed words I am repeating is strange,
As if the language has lost its way and can't get back.
The sound of the pencil scratching the tablet is strange,
As is the ticking of my watch, and the friction of my breath.
The shadow on the floor, the painting, the shelf of books,
The instruments leaning in the corner, the music on the stand -

These are what is strange.
All the familiar tackle and gear is suddenly adrift.
Where once there were simple signs and trustworthy tools now lie
A clutch of question marks, riddles, enigmatic fragments,
The scattered artifacts of a foreign life.

I read once how people who had suffered a stroke,
Who had lost the power to make sense with words,
Learned to speak again by singing.
Somehow the part of the brain which had come undone
Could find the way again with the help of a song.
It didn't matter what song it was, any song would do:
"Mairsy Doats", "When Irish Eyes", "A Mighty Fortress".
It was the singing which mattered.
Although so much was ruined a song remained,
And it was enough to begin again.
As little as this
"Mares eat oats, and does eat oats, and little lambs eat ivy,
When Irish eyes are smiling, all the world is bright and gay,
Did we in our own strength confide, our striving would be losing,"
If this is all a person had at hand
Then as little as this could be enough.

O Lord, open my lips and my mouth shall sing
"Stardust", "The Streets of Laredo", "Itsy Bitsy Spider",
"Away in A Manger", "For All the Saints",
And among all this that is so suddenly strange,
Let these songs be enough
To teach me to pray.

III.

One is named Phillip and he washes car windows but I haven't seen him for about six weeks now so maybe he went back to school. Phillip always came up to you looking like he was so FRUSTRAT-ED he might walk away before you even said yes or no.

Another is named Sam he washes car windows too Sam said he ran printing presses told me the names of different kinds and different processes but that was before now he lives at the Tillman shelter You have family here? The shelter's my family. Hard, hard hands, and a soft, soft hand-shake.

There's the young woman who always has a child in her arms the woman always looks dreamy with fatigue as if her eyes were focused somewhere else the child always looks healthy and alert and her hair is tipped with beads in the paper once someone wrote about the different names the woman goes by on 53rd St. once I saw her get out of a new car someone else was driving.

On 57th St. there is Ricky who sells pens he gets urgent with people who say they only have large bills and asks them to get change Ricky asks real hard when he says PLEASE and it sounds as if he is saying much more than that but if he said it with any word but PLEASE people would be too scared.

There's another man tall and thin I don't know his name who usually sits nearby he has worked this street for several years I know it used to be he would talk about food for his family but I don't hear him say that any more sometimes in the late afternoon I see Ricky and the tall man up on 55th St. sitting in a doorway where people going to restaurants pass by.

Outside the Walgreen's there is a heavy middle-aged woman weaving and staggering who sings and whistles and laughs and jingles coins she calls out invitations to men as they walk but I've never seen anybody answer.

There's also standing by the bank a man who sells a newspaper written by homeless people in the city usually it has a lot of poems in it he wears an identification card with his name and his picture I asked him if he had a poem in the paper and he said no not yet but maybe someday.

These are my neighbors whom I see most days often they offer a blessing as we pass whether I speak or not whether I say yes or no to what they ask it has taken me a long time to learn to stop and talk because I do not want to be embarrassed because I have nothing to say.

Now that would be a good trade:

 I could share some of what's in my pocket,
And they could share some of what's on their minds,
And maybe someday I'd learn to talk like a real person,
Like someone who talks to God.

Teach me to pray, I pray.

IV.

This bus runs twenty-four hours
Back and forth across town.
All day and all night from the museum to the airport
It will shudder and hiss and lurch and grind,
East to West, West to East, right to left, left to right,
A finger moving across a page of the Book,
Written on brick and asphalt, glass and concrete.
For the price of a ride you may sit down,
Open the scroll of the city and read.

The Book is infinite and inexhaustible.
A Book of Books holding together
What Nothing Else Can Hold.A Book of Beginnings, a Book of Unveiling,
A Book of Not Yet, and Now.
The bus makes a sucking wind to turn the pages,
Words swirl and scrape along the street,
Pile into corners, compose themselves again
Into another fragment of What Cannot Be Said.
Countless Books open and close;
On a given day you cannot say
Which ones it will be.
Today it is the Book of the Churches,
And today the Book of Murals,
And today the Book of Whoever Speaks to You.
The Book of the Churches reads:

St. Thomas the Apostle, Augustana,
The shell of St. Charles Lwanga,
New Philadelphia Church, True Love Missionary Baptist.

He spoke as if his mouth were full.
Crowded there like large round rocks,
Each word had to be found with his tongue
And pushed out into the air.
The Book of Whoever Speaks to You reads:
"You'd...think...the...Goddam
BUS...woulda...COME...sooner...huh?
fucking...weather...ME, I'M goin...home...
sleep...go to...that...JOB...go...home..."

Christ Tabernacle, and a church with no name,
but a dark skinned Jesus with outstretched arms.

"HATE that...job...can't...stand...that...
JOB...twelve years...in that...place...can't...
quit...for nine, ten...maybe...ELEVEN...years...more...
ELEVEN YEARS...I...can't stand it...CHRIST...moving...stuff...
around the floor...like...I'm...stupid...or somethin...

"The Book of Murals reads:
        LOVE   GOD   GOD
                                 IS
        LOVE   LOVE

Visitation Community Center & Thrift Shop,
Visitation, St. Basil Parish, St. Gall.

"I'd like to go...to...Minnesota...live by...one of them...
LAKES...fish...all day...all night...just...FISH...
I'd do it...that...tells you how...much...I like...
FISHIN...don't it?...you ever...live...there?
how...COLD...does it...get?...too...cold...HERE...
HATE this...weather...ANY kind...of...fish...
I don't...care..."

WE ARE HOPE FOR THE FUTURE
WE PROMISE 2-U YOU OUR LOVE

Julia Gay Memorial Church, Mount Vernon Missionary Baptist,
Holy Spiritual Temple, Kindest United House of Prayer.

"Look...they GOT...some...guy..see THAT...
handcuffs...bet...HE'S...mad...hands up...behind...
his...BACK...gotta...GUN...on'im..put'im...in the...car...
take'im...to jail...can't shake...this...damn...COLD...

Holy Life Tabernacle Church,
1st St. Peter Baptist, Jesus Church.

Door of Hope Rescue Mission.

YOUR SOUL IS BEAUTIFUL
FREEDOM FOR EVERYONE, LIFE FOR ALL

"Another one...over...there...a...LADY...
driver...they caught a...LADY...driving...bet..
you're glad...it's not your...WIFE...huh?
You...married?...not me...buddy...oh...NO...
You gotta...car?...your...wife...DRIVE?
drive you...CRAZY...you...mean...HA!'

I AM IN YOUR SOUL
IT IS GOOD TO BE HERE

GOD IN YOU

"Six...weeks...no...I...ain't seen...no...DOCTOR...
won't...do no...GOOD...fucking ASTHMA...huh?
I...just...COUGH...what you gonna...DO?
here's my...stop...bye pal...good...talking...to ya."

All Nations Pentecost Assembly,
Life Center Church of Universal Awareness,
Church of the Good Shepherd.

East to West, West to East,
Right to left, left to right,
A finger moves across the page.
Who is adequate to read such Books?
Who is adequate to hold them together?

Teach...me...to...pray...I...pray...

V.

This table is reason enough for endless thanks:

For all those who have sat around it,
For the gifts offered upon it,
For the stories told within the glow of its power.
If there is anything holy, then this table is.
If there is any sacrament, it can be nothing more
Than what has been given and received here.
Grace comes to be eaten and drunk;
We sit down at the altar of God.

The altar is there, too, and there, and there, and there.
This is its deep mystery:
The altar of God is made of chipped formica, straw matting;
It is a bowl in the hand, a cloth upon the ground.
The Bread of Heaven is corn, rice, beans, groundnut,

Manioc, potato, melon, olives, barley, grapes.
There, upon every table, the first truth is told;
There, upon every table, Body to body.

At this table join us
With all those who sit at table,
Whatever the table might be.
Here alone is reason enough for endless thanks,
And still there is more, gift upon gift.
At this table open our eyes to see.
At this table, Bread of Justice, Bread of Peace,
Teach us through what we do here, how to pray.

ENDNOTES

1. Soren Kierkegaard, *Concluding Unscientific Postscript*, David F. Swenson and Walter Lowrie, trans.(Princeton: Princeton University Press, 1968) p. 97.
2. Perry D. LeFevre, *Radical Prayer: Contemporary Interpretations* (Chicago: Exploration Press, 1982), p. 77.
3. *Radical Prayer*, p. 78.
4. *Radical Prayer*, p. 78.
5. *Radical Prayer*, p 78.
6. *Radical Prayer*, p. 85.
7. *Radical Prayer*, p. 93.
8. Gerard Manley Hopkins, "In honour of St. Alphonsus Rodriguez,Laybrother of the Society of Jesus," in *The Poems of Gerard Hopkins*, 4th Edition, W.H. Gardiner and N.H. MacKenzie, editors (London: Oxford University Press, 1967), p. 106.
9. *Radical Prayer*, p. 92.

Part II

HUMAN DEVELOPMENT

**Since God is Everywhere, Listen to the Language
of Events and Relationships**

CHAPTER V

The American Chalk Circle: Whose Child Is This?

by Bonnie J. Miller-McLemore

In "The Caucasion Chalk Circle," playwright Bertolt Brecht refashions an ancient Chinese folktale about the contested fate of a child. As revolutionaries assassinate a hated ruler, all those in his serfdom flee. The infant son of the pompous king is simply abandoned—first by the queen obsessed with the survival of her wardrobe, then by court physicians whose concern is motivated only by fear of the king's punishment, and then finally by the nurse whose care extends just up to the limits of her enslavement and no farther. The nurse hands the child to a servant girl, Grusha, simply asking her to "hold it a moment," before she herself flees, never to return.

The others, seeing the child in Grusha's arms urge her to put the child down. "Better put him down, I tell you. I'd rather not think what'd happen to anybody who's seen with that child. . . . They'll kill each other off, whole families at a time. Let's go. . . .If he had the plague it couldn't be worse. . . . You are a fool—just the kind that always gets put upon." Grusha can only mutter the obvious: "He's waking up . . . . The nurse asked me to hold him a moment . . . He hasn't got the plague. He looks at me! He's human!"[1] Still, she puts the sleeping child down, covers him with a blanket, starts away, and then runs for her life.

A child is left behind in its imaginary circle. Will anyone enter such a circle? With what consequences?

In the last several decades, the circle around children of the United States has contracted. Children have been justifiably identified as a source of women's oppression and "put down." Motherhood specifically, but fatherhood also, is a highly risky business these days.

However, while everyone proclaims "family values" in this election year for their own purposes, the real problems of mothers, fathers, and children get quickly brushed aside. Vice-president Quayle's recent equation of a "poverty of values" among the Murphy Browns of society and the Los Angeles riots illustrates the absurdity and damage of oversimplification. It is not clear that we as an American public have fully grasped the nature of the problems. Or more precisely, in political and religious discussions, people drift toward two-sided solutions, as the abortion debate exemplifies all too well.

When family life emerged as a compelling issue during the past two decades, evaluations quickly became polarized into "two competing and often warring camps," according to sociologist David Popenoe,

> On the one side, was the right-wing "moral majority," whose religiously based opinion . . . was that family decline was the equivalent of moral decay and was seriously weakening the very fiber of the nation. On the other side were some left-wing groups, especially radical feminist groups, who regarded family decline as a positive human achievement because it meant the decline of patriarchal tyranny and the continued liberation of the individual.[2]

Those in "mainline" churches and in theological education stand somewhere between these two positions. Few would want a simple return to the "traditional" or, more exactly, modern family—that is, the working father and domestic mother raising children—and fewer still the complete demise of the family. But exactly what theology has to offer from this important vantage point has not been seriously discussed. Rather than sitting in silence, those in mainline congregations must ask their own questions: What kind of family models should replace the tried and true ways of structuring the mother-father team that no longer work? What does a family type look like that does not exploit and depend so heavily on women? How do we get men involved? What further social, political, economic, and cultural changes are necessary to help families flourish?

From my own feminist theological perspective, we need to retain both the essentiality of woman's liberation and the centrality of children's vitality. Any rehabilitation of the family must incorporate the wisdom of the women's movement which exposed the family as a crucible for the reproduction of male domination and made clear the destructive effects of patriarchal power on women and children. At the same time, failure to rehabilitate the family must confront the faces of the children in the broken family circle. We must redefine the parameters of American circles of care for children. As a society, we need to broaden the circle.

Broadening the circle involves, but is not limited to, careful descriptive analysis of what is happening to mothers, fathers, and children and renewal of related theological language and concepts. This essay is an initial attempt to follow this two-fold agenda. While theologians cannot match the rigorous analysis of contemporary social scientists, we can use it to reconsider religious and cultural images of family. Theologians cannot determine the direction of future public policy. But we can reconsider the meanings of work, love, and human achievement that inform policies and shape culture. As much as we need adequate public policies, tax, education, and divorce reform, family-friendly work places and cities, we also need to reconstruct religious images of fatherhood, motherhood, self-sacrifice, and fulfillment.

In the family debate, many have latched on to another two-sided interpretation: either the family is "just changing" or the family is "declining." An introduction to a symposium on new books on the family sets examples of this polarization side by side: Sanford Dornbusch and Myra Strober, editors of *Feminism, Children, and the New Families*, argue, "the American family is changing, but then it always seems to be changing. It is stable in its flexibility, its adaptation to changing social conditions."[3] But in David Popenoe's opinion, "the family . . . is in *decline* . By this I mean that the institution of the family is growing weaker; it is losing social power and social functions, losing influence over behavior and opinion, and generally becoming less important in life."[4]

Both of these judgments capture a certain truth. On one hand, some family structures and functions have declined. The heightened individualism and technical rationality have had an unrelenting impact on all social institutions, including families, weakening attachments between spouses and between parents and children and eroding the cohesion, stability, and life span of families.

But on the other hand, the "stable" family of previous decades stabilized itself at the expense of many within its boundaries, particularly women but also children. As awareness of the physical, sexual, and emotional abuse hidden in families grows, we have to ask, is this the decline of a facade—the facade of a healthy, harmonious family institution whose power to dictate and control behavior and opinion was indeed questionable at several serious points? As Friedrich Engels noted in1884 in the *The Origin of the Family, Private Property and the State*, a change in the family of his era might be of clear benefit, especially for women.[5]

However, when either the "decline" or "just changing" position is taken alone as the sole, facile analysis, it reduces the complexity of the situation. The use of decline language reveals serious blind spots. In Popenoe's case, he asserts that decline is not "necessarily bad."[6] But the dictionary definition itself—"to turn from a straight course" or "to stoop to what is unworthy"—proves otherwise. The term hides a pejorative, moralistic judgment. In a time when people struggle to find appropriate language to describe evolving commitments and relationships and need new words, people should proceed cautiously in the blanket use of any simple term like decline. At the same time, more is happening to the family than change alone.

Popenoe's assertion that decline is not necessarily bad reveals a second important point. Decay of the family is one thing; its meaning another. As already illustrated, its meaning will differ for different individuals and groups.

The forces against parenting, mothering in particular, are formidable: the pressures of an economy that discounts the unpaid work of home and family, the economic vulnerabilities of all women who choose to become mothers, and the additional burdens of racism and classism; the political aloofness of a conservative government that refuses to see the changes that have happened in the lives of women, children, and families; the social tensions that keep the old norms about a woman's place in the home alive in the collective subconscious; the emotional turmoil of being a mother in a world that at once idealizes and devalues the work mothers do; the formidable giants of materialism, media, and drugs that war over the minds of the young; the corporate time clock that quickens the pace of life along "future shock" predictions; and the practical complications of sustaining one's own life and supporting the life of another. "Better put him down, I tell you. . . . You are a fool—just the kind that always gets put upon." Who will enter such a circle? Given these adverse forces, choosing to have a child in today's world is an heroic act.

What about fathers? Have they entered the circle? Despite the increasing acceptance of men taking charge of child care, not many men spend much more time with their children than their fathers did and even fewer plan their lives around marriage and family as women continue to do.[7] If the divorce rate remains high and nonmarital childbearing continues its upward trend, sixty percent of the children born in the 1990s will live in families with a single parent before age sixteen.[8] Of these families, custodial fathers still remain a rare breed. Despite changes in the nature of custody decisions, many fathers do not request custody, and most children remain in the care of their mothers.[9] Of these children, only three-fifths receive any financial support and many of these gradually lose contact with the nonresidential father. Of the children who receive support, the amount paid averages about $235 a month, an amount that does not cover an adequate portion of the real costs.[10] In this regard, it is important to note that female-headed households are exceptionally vulnerable to poverty for a wide variety of reasons—the sexual economic discrimination of all women, paid roughly one-third less in salary, wages, and benefits than men, the built-in conflicts between work structures and child rearing, the costs of child care, the compounding problems of racial discrimination.[11]

Some men do not have the money; others pay little or no child support "because they can get away with it."[12] But more fairly, men have been heralded as the family provider for too long, a role that keeps them out of the circle with too little reward. In the hearts of men, the demands of economic sustenance apart from emotional intimacy have gradually eroded desires to care for children. The gender-based division of labor in the family, compounded by the general devaluation of the nurturing role, have made it difficult, if not impossible, for men to prize foremost attachments and commitments to children, with or apart from financial support.

The forces against children and childhood are equally complex. Simply consider, says Richard Louv, author of *Childhood's Future*, all the "firsts" faced by many of today's children:

> They are the first day-care generation; the first truly multicultural generation; the first generation to grow up in the electronic bubble, the environment defined by computers and new forms of television; the first post-sexual revolution generation; the first generation for which nature is more abstraction than reality; the first generation to grow up in new kinds of dispersed, decon-

centrated cities, not quite urban, rural, or suburban.[13]
Louv believes these "firsts" combine to further the growing distance between adults and children. Contact between adults and children, instilling in young the wisdom of age and instilling in the old the vitality of youth, has seriously degenerated.

The problems are not limited to declining contact but actually concern the bottom-line. Our national allocation of financial resources reflects the extent to which we fail to value children and nurture. While America has made significant advances in caring for the elderly, something is awry when we spend 24 percent of our budget on the old and just 4 percent on families with children, when we spend $100 billion on health care for the elderly and just $14 billion on children, when we underwrite multiple heart-bypass surgery to 70-year-olds and fail to provide prenatal care for poor women.[14] As Marian Wright Edelman claims, we are "on the verge of losing" our children—Black, white, Latino, Native American, and other children—to the dangers of "drugs, violence, too-early parenthood, poor health and education, unemployment, family disintegration," and ultimately to the "meaninglessness of a culture that rewards greed and guile and tells them life is about getting rather than giving."[15]

A child is left behind. Who will enter such a circle? Grusha does not stay away. At the last moment, she returns, just to see if the child is still there. In the story teller's words,

> As she was standing between courtyard and gate,
> She heard or she thought she heard a low voice calling;
> The child called to her,
> Not whining, but calling quite sensibly,
> At least so it seemed to her.
> "Woman," it said, "help me."
> And it went on, not whining, but saying quite sensibly:
> "Know, woman, he who hears not a cry for help
> But passes by with troubled ears will never hear
> The gentle call of a lover nor the blackbird at dawn
> Nor the happy sigh of the exhausted grape-picker as the angelus rings."
>
> She dares to walk toward the child for one more look,
> Only to sit with him for a moment or two,
> Only till someone should come,
> Its mother, perhaps, or anyone else. . . .
> Only till she would have to leave, for the danger was too great,
> The city was full of flame and crying. . . .
> Terrible is the seductive power of goodness! . . .
> A long time she sat with the child
> Till evening came, till night came, till dawn came.
> Too long she sat, too long she saw
> The soft breathing, the little fists,
> Till toward morning the temptation grew too strong
> And she rose, and bent down, and sighing, took the child
> And carried it off . . . .

> Like plunder she took it to herself
> Like a thief she crept away.[16]

The rest of the tale is neither naive or sentimental. Grusha struggles to survive and take care of the child. Within her own country, she flees death by revolutionaries who might discover the child's rightful lineage; beyond her town, she is ostracized as an unwed mother, thrown out of her own brother's house when he and her sister-in-law cannot bear the shame Grusha represents.

Finally, she faces a second circle, the actual chalk circle—an account familiar to those who know Solomon's judgment in I Kings 3: 16-27. When the revolution and risk subsides, the queen decides she wants her son back. A judge designs a test to determine the true mother—a chalk circle out of which both women must try to pull the child. Grusha lets go. Standing aghast at her loss, she pleads and the test is repeated. She lets go again. "I brought him up! Shall I tear him to pieces? I can't do it!"[17] Like the mother in I Kings, Grusha is torn between the desire to divide the child to have him and the knowledge that the child's own life depends upon letting go.

In the American chalk circle, many are more like Grusha in the first act's more invisible circle; many are torn between the desire to have a life of their own and the knowledge that the child's very life depends upon their grabbing hold. The mother in a Cathy cartoon hands Zenith to the father, "Now Daddy will play with Zenith while Mommy works in her home office!" Handing Zenith back Dad protests, "Daddy's been out of his office for two hours! Mommy was supposed to do her work in the morning!" Mom, handing Zenith back to Dad, says, "Mommy spent the morning scraping play-doh out of her computer keyboard!" Dad, handing Zenith back to Mom, says "It isn't Daddy's fault that mommy is disorganized!" "Daddy hasn't tried to conduct business with a two-and-a-half-year-old hanging from his neck!!" The last caption says: "Another couple crosses the fine line between care-giving and guilt-giving."

However, in contrast to the Cathy's guilt-ridden author, mothers and fathers today feel guilty not so much because mothers and fathers are guilty—most parents are doing their best—but because parents care in a context that lacks the necessary supportive structures and ideologies that foster care-giving. As a society, we tend to forget, as John MacMurray observes, "If nobody intends [the child's] survival and acts with intention to secure it, he cannot survive . . . . He can live only through other people and in dynamic relation with them."[18] Parents care in a society that denies the core dependencies of human nature and nurture, at the center of which stands parent and child.

Biblical images of motherhood and fatherhood are in sorry need of attention. Sermonic interpretations of the story in I Kings tend to elevate Solomon and do little more than patronize the harlot women. And the actual mother in the story of Solomon has become the epitome of the self-sacrificing mother who forfeits her own needs in order that the child might live, while father Abraham willingly sacrifices his child Isaac out of loyalty to his God. Either image, valuable in itself, when taken to its extreme and instituted into rigid roles and structures of work and love, has directly contributed to the devastation of many modern families. Today we have fathers who sacrifice their families for their work and mothers who sacrifice themselves for their children. Powerful images of the "good mother" forbid other loves besides children; powerful images of masculinity forbid passionate fatherhood. Both endanger the vitality of the institutions of motherhood and fatherhood.

The wisdom of Solomon is less the wisdom of a king and more the wisdom of a mother. His so-called wisdom rests upon the wisdom of the mother whose "heart yearns" for the child (I Kings 3: 26). And Brecht's text stretches the wisdom of the biological mother to the folly of the nonbiological mother, the one who hesitates. The simple willingness to pick up a sleeping, waking child, to look in its face and see that it is human—a "heart that yearns"—is critical and need not depend upon an innate genetic maternal bond.

Anyone can have a "heart that yearns" and more people, especially men, must. For, the ties that bind are not bound by blood. Dominant Western idealizations of motherhood have exaggerated the inherent powers of maternal instinct, assuming the nursing mother knows just what to do. Such ideals have failed to cultivate in each person broader "parental instincts"—to borrow Sally McFague's term.[19] To give and secure life are communal obligations for the survival of all. Our parental instincts morally oblige everyone to enter the circle and extend the instinct of life preservation beyond individual lives to the lives of the child and to the life of the world.

But as Grusha's saga proves, it takes more than a "heart that yearns." Mothers have been silent for too long. The absence of maternal voices has kept the hardships of care hidden from view. If the mothers in the biblical text could talk, we might discover important realities about children and the duties of care. Children are immensely more valuable, more vulnerable, and a lot more work than our cultural imagination has conceded and our economies and politics would like to acknowledge. These harlot mothers might tell us of their deep yearnings for the child and of their moments of desire to destroy it; they might tell of their deep, contradictory love and hate toward this dependent, vulnerable, valuable child. They might describe the powerful dynamic of all real care—the intricate, complicated dance between self-sacrifice and self-survival.

Over "Cathy" I prefer the honest wisdom of "For Better or For Worse": The father returns from work to cradle the new baby, "MMMM—There's nothing sweeter than the smell of a freshly bathed baby! There's nothing more compelling than the look in a little child's eyes! What words can describe the intense and special feeling a mother has after being at home with her baby all day?" "GET ME OUR OF HERE!"

The ethical dynamics of care are more complicated than the theories of men have known or understood. Love, particularly the love between parent and child, involves ample sacrifice certainly, but self-sacrifice must never become the ideal. Even in the earliest moments of nurture a mother must receive something back through the infant's eyes, or sacrifice becomes a noisy gong or a clanging cymbal. A parent cannot give to children unless the giving is alleviated and countered by contrasting moments of self-gratification. Equally critical, when the dependent child cannot give back, the ability to sacrifice in response to a child's needs depends upon a broader familial, social, and cultural context of give-and-take. A parent cannot give unless the giving is refreshed and relieved by the support of another, whether spouse, neighbor, friend, relative, or stranger.

In other words, the self-giving necessary to care in dependent relationships is healthy and good only in a society in which caring is neither a compulsory experience nor an exploitative or oppressive one. Necessary, essential moments of sacrifice rest upon other necessary and essential moments in which a person's satisfaction is granted. And with a child who cannot give too much, too early, sacrifice needs others standing by until a later time of reciprocity. In the interlude, many hands must rock the cradle and share the burdens of dependence. Self-sacrifice, even that of Christ's, never rests on its own, alone, unaided, uninterrupted nor should it ever replace mutuality as the ultimate goal.

Parents and mothers in particular do better to admit and even affirm the hopes and needs they harbor both in relationship to their children and in regards to their own work. Erik Erikson is singular in his perceptive psychological analysis of this engagement between generations. A "mutuality" and an "ecology of mutual activation" between child and adult, youth and grandparent, young and old governs each stage of growth. The adult both gives *and* gets, and the child both gives *and* gets. A mutuality in which "one's self-interest is often, but not always, also the interest of the other" is interspersed with many moments of self-sacrifice. But they are "just that—moments in a process designed to end in mutual love."[20] Children operate as partners, albeit less adept and seasoned, in the practice of mutuality in its temporal dimension and development. This generativity allows the child to continue to grow; it expects the adult to do likewise. Theories of development that focus so essentially upon the child's progress, including Erikson's own theory, fail to consider adequately the immense coinciding, reciprocal changes in the adult, developments absolutely necessary for adequate care. If the mother and father do not balance their own interests with the work of parenting, if they do not grow with their children, the children will not prosper and flourish.

Little attention has gone to inevitable tension between moments of self-absorption and moments of self-giving that marks all genuine human work and love. Although for much of the race work remains forced drudgery in front of machines, brooms, words, or numbers, all persons deserve work that is a vital source of meaning and creativity. A sanctioned self-absorption of heart and mind—the kind of immersion in activity that children display when work and play and child are one—is a part of all meaningful work. If women, mothers in particular, are to have such creative work, they must be allowed self-absorption, uninterrupted by fleeting thoughts and guilt about caring for others, children or otherwise.

The term "good enough mother" was first used in psychoanalytic object relations theory to depict responses to a child's needs that include a rough balance of empathic failures and successes to ensure a child's healthy emotional development.[21] But the frequent use of this term in psychodynamic interpretations seldom considers what it takes to become a "good enough mother." Moreover, there is no such person as a "good enough mother" without a "good enough family" in a "good enough community."

Mainline congregations have no investment in defending the traditional or modern family hung up about good enough mothering. Congregations should develop a commitment to the ideal of a "good enough family" in a "good enough community." The wording of the latter suggests the limits of defending some one perfect family form without losing the important idea that strong families are critical and that we need serious conversation about the parameters of what makes a family "good enough."

Sustaining a "good enough family" in a "good enough community" requires supporting families in which partners share mutual responsibility for the public and domestic aspects of family life; and it requires supporting adequate social, cultural support systems for family functioning. An adequate understanding of a "good enough family" begins with a reconstruction of the ethic of Christian love in which equal regard, rather than self-sacrifice, reigns. A "truly democratic gender and kinship order," according to Judith Stacey, that does not favor "male authority, heterosexuality, a particular division of labor, or a singular household or parenting arrangement" has become thinkable for the first time in our history.[22] An ethic of equal regard grounds the mutuality required of a truly generative family of many forms and structures. Genuine generativity is the bottom line, not a particular family form or structure.

When children are involved, the "parental emergency" of having children initially demands flexible, somewhat differentiated gender roles and activities. But persons involved in the work of child rearing cannot sustain the necessary self-sacrifice apart from other avenues of self-fulfillment and from the help of supportive public structures. An ethic of mutuality calls for greater male responsibility for care of familial covenants, including the care of children. It is wrong to recommend the mother-father team in a culture in which such a team continues to mean that women do most of the real labor to make it work. And such an ethic assumes more explicit expectations about the gradual responsibilities and contributions of children to the work of family.

This position also challenges a cultural ethos that provides little sanction, status, or time for either the parental emergency or for the work involved in sustaining the necessary dependencies of family life in general. Equal regard can only be sustained in a social network that recognizes and provides for the demands and sacrifices involved in families, from raising children to caring for the aging. Covenant in the biblical family, according to Walter Brueggeman, includes child-raising as only one among a multitude of essential relational commitments—intergenerational, marital, sibling, and the larger network of the entire household and dependent, marginal persons.[23] Today we must figure in several new relational commitments, such as stepfamilies, child care givers, work-related commitments, and so forth. Child raising is crucial but it is the vitality of these other covenants that make child rearing possible at all.

"And now I'll tell you," explains Grusha when she is reunitied with her lover in the final act: She first picked up the child "because on that Sunday, I got engaged to you. And so he's a child of love. Let us dance."[24] Their love, the love they shared, opened her ears to the child's cry. Without the love of others, we cannot hear the cries of our children.

And "she who hears not a cry for help, but passes by . . . will never hear the gentle call of a lover nor the blackbird at dawn nor the happy sign of the exhausted grape-picker as the Angelus rings." He who hears not the "soft breathing" and sees not the "little fists" of the one in the midst of us fails the litmus test of human giving and caring. "Whoever receives one such child" receives more and lives more abundantly. One who has cared for a child— dressing, nursing, feeding, cleaning, wiping, clipping, cutting, brushing, guarding, protecting, reprimanding, instructing, watching, following, listening, mediating—one who has seen the face of God in a child stands to gain new empathy for the other, other children, other people, the oppressed and those in need.

Caring labor for another, practiced over and over, teaches something nameless that is nonetheless essential to life and living. As a religious people and as a nation, we are carefully, cautiously dancing around the circle. The test lies before us.

NOTES AND REFERENCES

1. Bertolt Brecht, "The Caucasian Chalk Circle," in *Seven Plays*, ed. with an introduction by Erick Bently (New York: Grove Press, 1961), p. 519.
2. David Popenoe, *Disturbing the Nest: Family Change and Decline in Modern Societies* (New York: Aldine De Gruyter, 1988), p. 31.
3. Sanford M. Dornbusch and Myra H. Strober, eds., *Feminism, Children, and the New Families*, p. 12. Cited by Joan Aldous "Symposium: Families by The Book," *Comtemporary Sociology* 20, No. 6 (November 1991): 660-667.
4. Popenoe, *Disturbing the Nest*, p. xii.
5. Friedrich Engels, *The Origin of the Family, Private Property and the State* (London: Penquin, 1972 [1884]).
6. Popenoe, *Disturbing the Nest*, p. 9
7. Arlie Hochschild, with Anne Machung, *The Second Shift: Working Parents and the Revolution at Home* (New York: Viking, 1989), pp. 2-4; Rosemary Curran Barciauskaas and Debra Berry Hull, *Loving and Work: Reweaving Women's Public and Private Lives* (Bloomington, Ind.: Meyer-Stone Books, 1989), pp. 39-40; see also J. H. Pleck, "The Work-Family Problem: Overloading the System," in *Outsiders on the Inside: Women and Organizations*, B. L. Furisha and B. H. Goldman, eds. (Englewood Clifs, N.J.: Prentice-Hall, 1981), pp. 239-54.
8. Frank F. Furstenberg, Jr., and Andrew J. Cherlin, *Divided Families: What Happens to Children When Parents Part* (Cambridge, Mass.: Harvard University Press, 1991), p. 11.

9. Claude S. Fisher, "The Dispersion of Kinship Ties in Modern Society: Contemporary Data and Historical Speculation," *Journal of Family History* 7 (1982): 353-375.

10. Furstenberg and Cherlin, *Divided Families*, p. 50.

11. See Pamela D. Couture, *Blessed are the Poor? Women's Poverty, Family Policy, and Practical Theology* (Nashville: Abingdon, 1991).

12. Furstenberg and Cherlin, *Divided Families*, p. 60.

13. Richard Louv, *Childhood's Future* (Boston: Houghton Mifflin, 1990), p. 5.

14. Sylvia Ann Hewlett, *When the Bough Breaks: The Cost of Neglecting Our Children* (New York: Basic Books, 1991).

15. Marian Wright Edelman, *The Measure of Our Success: A Letter to My Children and Yours* (Boston: Beacon, 1992), p. 15.

16. Brecht, "The Caucasian Chalk Circle," pp. 520-21.

17. Ibid., p. 585.

18. John MacMurray, *Persons in Relation* (London: Faber and Faber, 1961), pp. 49, 51.

19. See Sally McFague, *Models of God: Theology for an Ecological, Nuclear Age* (Philadelphia: Fortress, 1987), pp. 105, 119-20.

20. Christine E. Gudorf, "Parenting, Mutual Love, and Sacrifice," in *Women's Consciousness and Women's Conscience: A Reader in Feminist Ethics*, eds. Barbara Hilkert Andolsen, Christine E. Gudorf and Mary D. Pellauer (San Francisco: Harper & Row, 1985), pp. 184, 186.

21. See D. W. Winnicott, *Through Paediatrics to Psycho-Analysis* (London: Hogarth, 1958); *The Maturational Process and the Facilitating Environment* (New York: International University Press, 1965); and *Playing and Reality* (London: Tavistock, 1971); see also Bruno Bettelheim, *A Good Enough Parent: A Book on Child-Rearing* (New York: Vintage, 1987).

22. Judith Stacey, *Brave New Families: Stories of Domestic Upheaval in Late Twentieth Century America* (New York: Basic Books, 1990), p. 258.

23. See Walter Brueggeman, "The Covenanted Family: A Zone for Humanness," *Journal of Current Social Issues* 14, No. 1 (Winter 1977), pp. 18-23.

24. Brecht, "The Caucasian Chalk Circle," p. 586.

CHAPTER VI

Joseph Son of Jacob

by André LaCocque

To Perry LeFevre, a father-figure to many, a friend to all.

The story of Joseph in Genesis 37-50 starts by introducing a brat, who cannot keep his mouth shut when, indeed, it would avoid him and others a lot of trouble, and even perhaps save his life. According to tradition, he talks too much not just once but twice, in full knowledge of possible consequences. Paradoxically, his attempts to increase his own importance in the eyes of others attracts upon himself the hatred of his siblings and the rebuke of his father. The more he tells about his offensive dreams, the more he embarrasses everyone and endangers his own existence. Here there is a sort of sinister spiral or vicious circle in which Joseph seems to be inextricably enmeshed.

In fact, the whole story is built with taut ambiguities and woven with extremes in an uneasy coexistence. The father's reaction to his son's bragging is itself a mixture of reprobation and pride. He chides Joseph but we learn that he also keeps his son's blusters at heart (Gen. 37.11). As for Joseph, he has little inclination toward his brothers, but he goes out of his way (37.14b,17) to inquire about their well being (37.13,16...). These young men themselves are presented as a mixture of viciousness, cruelty, blood thirst, but also of straightforwardness, simplicity, self-forgetfulness. Tension is maintained from start to finish in the novella because, after Joseph has been sold as a slave to slave traders, everyone at home thinks that he is dead, when in fact he is alive and well. There is irony, even dark humor, in the fact that Jacob mourns the lad when, as a matter of fact, he need not weep but rejoice.

Similarly, there is irony in the roller coaster-like destiny of Joseph, who starts in life with the conviction of being immune from the ills that generally plague the rest of humanity. From the time of the fateful encounter in a place called Dothan with his brothers to whom he was commissioned to show kindness and benevolence, he is tossed from success to dismal dereliction, from general oblivion to fame, from there again to pit, and eventually to consummate elevation. Fittingly in that sort of story, from which the miraculous is banned (obvious parallels are found in the stories of Ruth and Esther, the latter in clear dependence on Joseph's saga), even God's presence and action, so central a feature in the rest of the Ancestral narratives, become here highly ambiguous. True, we are told at times that "the Lord was with Joseph" (39.2,21), but such declarations are conspicuously rare and all in one chapter, so that the reader's suspicion is aroused that we probably are dealing with pious additions to an otherwise purposefully secular discourse.[1]

Generically, these striking ups and downs in Joseph's life, these alternatives of descent and ascent, humiliation and glorification, belong to the hellenistically influenced literary genre of the novella.[2] A major theme in this *Gattung* is *peripety*[3], i.e., then reversal of fortune, the unexpected and paradoxical outcome of an action. In the story of Joseph (as also in the book of Esther, for example), peripeties abound. Much of the authorial religious trust and faith finds in this theme its pole of investment. In its rebounds, history reveals divine care and concern. There is no need for the direct interventions of a *deus ex machina*. Any "miracle" would dissolve the tension intrinsic to the plot and bring the story to a radically different level of communication and message. Furthermore, much of the power of the story resides in the deeply rooted reader's empathy with a character, though described without complacency, who goes through the vicissitudes of life as through the purifying crucible of initiatory rites of passage, armed only with his/her own courage and conviction of being "elected."

True, divine participation in the hero's fate is not ignored, but it is important that God's presence to Joseph is *mediated* by his dealings with the Patriarch Jacob/Israel. In the absence of his father, Joseph in Egypt lives with only a dimmed and veiled divine presence. Only when Jacob is about to come down to Egypt to join his son is there a theophany (directly at the benefit of Jacob and indirectly on behalf of Joseph) and a sudden multiplication of references to God by Joseph (45.4-8; 50.15-20). E.M. McGuire has grasped that indissolubility in Joseph's eyes of the persons of God and his father. McGuire writes, "[Joseph] consistently and graciously defers to both father and God in questions of authority, precedence, and definitive interpretations."[4]

In that respect, as already alluded to above, the theological declarations of Genesis 39.1-5 display a strictly authorial point of view.[5] Before it can be said with this chapter that "The Lord was with Joseph," — a declaration that, strictly speaking, belongs to the denouement, — it is important to follow Joseph into his initial general oblivion (40.23). If chapter 39 were not an authorial set-aside, the motif of providential governance at this point of the story would be self-defeating. We are shown in the following chapter (ch. 40), that Joseph was forgotten, not just by one individual, in the person of Pharaoh's cupbearer, but by all, including God for all practical purposes.

In a stark contrast, however, there is one who is not contaminated by universal obliviousness, namely his father (37.11, and passim). It is only *through* that human medium that divine remembrance is channelled down and made known to the reader. Joseph in the pit where his brothers threw him, and on the rim of which they are even able to eat and converse as if nothing happened (37.25), or Joseph in the oubliette where he is equally consigned to oblivion, holds to life only by one thread, whose other end is in his father's hands. Whether one or both of them are unconscious of it does not weaken the bond between them. In the story of Joseph, God speaks exclusively through the channel of the father - son relationship. It is the key to the Joseph novella. Statistically, there are no less than 92 occurrences of the word "father" in the chapters 37-50 of Genesis. Nowhere else in Hebrew Scriptures do we find such a concentrated focus on fatherhood.[6]

Precisely this striking distinction of the biblical narrative calls for comparison with the Greek myth of Oedipus, that psychoanalysis since Sigmund Freud has selected as paradigmatic of the father and son relationship. The mythic view is as fascinating as the dizzy making emptiness of an abyss. The myth takes us to the contemplation of one of the most pessimistic interpretations of the generational gap. Not only is the gap naturally unbridgeable, but it manipulatively moves father and son into projects of infanticide, parricide, incest, self-inflicted mutilations, and consequently into guilt, loathe of self, contempt of others, suicide. Psychoanalytic hermeneutics finds in the Oedipus myth the golden key to the human psyche. Humans are by nature and destiny murderous, incestuous, sadistic, and masochistic. After the iconoclasts Galileo and Darwin, Freud destroys the last stronghold of human centeredness, the soul. The onslaught is powerfully overwhelming; it sweeps all obstacles on its way like a twister. Any objection to the theory will now sound like complacency, inability to look squarely at reality, self-indulgence — cravenness. Whoever may be his adversary, Freud, it seems, will always triumph, *precisely in the name of the guilt he has unmasked in all of us!*

Freud invincible? In the premises of his analysis, yes. In his deterministic conclusions, this remains to be seen. At issue is the possibility or impossibility to transcend the Oedipus complex. It is at this point that the story of Joseph is the most effective. It is, I contend, an anticipative response of sorts to Freud, on a par with the lucid absence of complacency in the attack. The generational gap is here also accepted as a fact (as well as sibling rivalry, an important dimension of the story that will not be dealt with here). But the gap is not all there is to know about the father - son (parent - child) relationship. It is not even the first thing to say in that relationship, and certainly not the last.

As in the correspondence of male and female according Genesis, father and son are first considered as one reality contemplated from two different vantage points. In Genesis 2 the "human" is one flesh seen either from the side of masculinity/convexity (the meaning of the Hebrew word *zakhar*), or from the side of femininity/ concavity (the meaning of the Hebrew word *neqebah*). In a striking parallel, Genesis 37 ff. present paternity - sonship (parenthood - childhood) as two aspects of one relation. In the novella, Jacob is envisaged strictly within his role of father for Joseph (or for Benjamin, Joseph's alter ego, as we shall see below); and Joseph is throughout seen as the son of Jacob/Israel. Were it not for this particularity, the story would make very little sense. The deepest creative ambiguity in the tale obtains through the *physical* separation between father and son, while *spiritually* [or depth- psychologically], communion between the two is what triumphs over all odds.

In Genesis 37-50, contrary to the Oedipus myth, there is no Joseph without Jacob — not only from the generational point of view — and there is no Jacob/Israel without Joseph! True, between father and son, Israelite tradition also acknowledges a process, albeit provisional, of distancing. In the Hebrew tale, it typically occurs when Joseph is seventeen (37.2)! But the separation, although combining the temporal and the spatial axes, is seen as a means towards a superior goal; it is transcended by the deeply rooted refusal of the protagonists to consider the distance as decisive and final.

Hebrew Scriptures thus start by affirming the bond between father and son. The Patriarchal/ Matriarchal stories that precede the novella of Joseph strongly emphasize this generational concatenation, although, no less than in the relation between genders, the succession of generations is imperilled by forces within/or beyond the family control. In the sagas of Abraham, Isaac, and Jacob, the obstacle is mainly biological: the potential mothers are barren or too old. In other words, engendering the future is never to be taken for granted. Childbirth is always a miracle. With the Joseph story we proceed one step further. Child rearing is also fraught with danger. The threat is multifarious. It comes from a doting father blind to his own favoritism,[7] from a brat unconscious of the enormity of his narcissism,[8] from his siblings intoxicated with their own destructive jealousy;[9] it comes from geographical, cultural, generational, distancing; from misconceptions, misunderstandings, false assumptions ... Such (unavoidable?) breaches, even when they reach their extreme limit as in the story of Jacob and Joseph are, however, incapable of putting asunder father and son as long as *both* do not cut the cord and break the unity. On the contrary, when this is not permitted to occur, they continue to share a *being* that is common to both.

Susan Niditch[10] summerizes for us the common features to both Jacob and Joseph, drawing her inspiration from the works of J.G. von Hahn (1876)[11], Otto Rank (1909)[12] and Lord Raglan (1934)[13]

- The hero is born from a formerly barren mother;
- "Difficulty in conception," the latter is "unusual" and fulfills a "prophecy of ascendance;"
- Father is related to mother;
- Life threatening forces surround hero;
- Hero "seeks service abroad;"
- Process of hero's maturation;
- "Triumphant homecoming" (variation in the story of Joseph);
- Hero "acknowledged by people" and "achieves rank and honor."

Also of particular interest to us is the notable absence of major themes present in the Oedipus myth, such as the royal or divine quality of the hero's parents; the "prophecy warning against birth" (e.g., because of danger of parricide); "hero abandoned;" "suckled by animals;" "hero takes [ultimate] revenge on his father;" "commits incest;" "murders his younger brother;"[14] etc. As Niditch writes, "The biblical composers deny themselves [these] outlet[s]; conflict in the Israelite family ends in peacemaking and harmony."[15]

The Joseph account once more affirms this ending. It is an end already present at the beginning, which remains operative throughout. This is conspicuous in the unity of destiny and being between father and son that, in the novella, falls victim to the "death" of Joseph which also implies the "minus-being" of Jacob. The mourning rites of the father (37.34) indicate that much. They consist in displaying all kinds of signs of the mourner's death. One throws dust upon one's head, as an acknowledgement of reverting to the dust of the earth, and one dons rags, which are symbolic of the disaffection for life and its vanities. Jacob refuses to be comforted and declares, "I am going down to the Sheol to the son of my grief" (37.35).

But, in the story, there is *peripeteia*: Joseph is not dead, and this entails that neither is Jacob. One of them goes up toward more and more being, toward plus-being, and therefore the other's going down to minus-being is untimely and ironic. Symbolically, the story juxtaposes in stark contrast the abundance in Egypt, thanks to Joseph's wisdom, and the famine that hits Canaan, now that Joseph is gone and that Jacob is the shadow of himself. Only when he is sure that Joseph lives, does "the spirit of Jacob revive" (45.27), and abundance is retrieved (47.12).

That is why, even when the text focuses on Joseph in Egypt and seems to forget about Canaan where Jacob resides, the father is never absent from the picture. The elevation of Joseph, and his earlier humiliations, must be read with Jacob/Israel in mind. Joseph's sufferings were his. And it does not belong only to artistic tension and "retardation" in the literary composition that the son of Jacob's glorification is *not* shared by him for a long time. It is tragic and properly abnormal for this conception of humanity that the father does not even know about his son's miraculous survival and astounding promotion. Were it the fate of all parent-child relationship, the story's dramatic tension would be considerably lessened. The tale of Joseph demands from its audience/ readership, not resignation and fatalism, but faith, hope, and trust: the parting of the ways between Jacob and Joseph is *not* a natural process, and it is *not* an end in itself. Separation here cannot be considered simply as a "healthy evolution," notwithstanding the fact that it does not remain without a profound effect on Joseph and on Jacob. As far as the father's personality is concerned, W. Lee Humphreys sums it up well in a concise formula. "A man of excesses becomes in time a man of reserve."[16] Conversely, no one will fail to see the enormous distance skillfully worked out by the poet between young Joseph and the great vizier of Egypt.

As soon as Joseph feels that the relationship with his family can be restored, he comes with a most significant statement to his brothers, "And now you see with your own eyes, and so does my brother Benjamin ... and you'll tell my father ... all you have seen; hurry, bring my father down here" (45.12-13). As McGuire writes, "As significant as the brothers' knowledge of him may be, that knowledge seems to have largely the function of bringing Jacob into Joseph's presence so that the father may at last truly see and hear his lost son"[17].

That declaration announces the denouement. The latter, once the literary device of retardation has been fully exploited, comes "in a contrastingly quick, staccato, phrases at 45.3."[18] At that point, the equilibrium in the shared being of father and son is restored. Then Jacob/Israel once again speaks of his death, but in a totally different spirit. "Bounteousness of my son Joseph alive! I'll go and see him before I die" (45.28), and, after the realization of his desire, "This time I can die now that I have seen your face, for you *are* alive!" (46.30).

The father's exclamation is an echo of the son's illogical but so meaningful cry, "I am Joseph! Is my father alive?" (45.3). His question in that place, at that moment, does not seem to make any sense after the dialogue that precedes with Judah, although Joseph's interjection does only echo his earlier pressing questions about Jacob's welfare in 43.7,27. Judah's eloquence, furthermore, has been precisely based upon the heart-wrenching evocation of the father Jacob, whose "life [or, soul, *nephesh*] is bound up in his [Benjamin's] life [*nephesh*]" (44.30). So that Joseph's ejaculation makes a lot of sense within the referential framework of the intimate and almost symbiotic relation between himself and his younger brother Benjamin. In this respect, let us note that one universal folkloric motif is the birth of twins in divine response to a barren woman's petition. In the case of Jacob and Esau, the motif is literally present; as regards Joseph and Benjamin, there is a mysterious sameness of the two. There is the same symbiotic attachment of Jacob with the one and the other, that makes them twins, even interchangeable.

Benjamin, also born from Rachel like Joseph, is so completely identified in the story with Joseph that he has no personality of his own. He is the alter ego of Joseph; he never acts or speaks of his own. He is entirely representative, symbolic, and substitutive. This is an important feature, as it shows another aspect of the father-and-son relationship whereby, against all "Oedipal" evidence, Benjamin does *not* leave the father, nor the father leave the son. Hence Joseph/ Benjamin duality evidences a dialectic relation with the father. Joseph is the son-that-goes-away; Benjamin is the son-that-stays, like in Jesus's parable. Also like in the parable, the one that goes, in a certain way remains home in the person of his sibling, and conversely the one who stays is in a certain way detached from the family moorings in the person of his prodigal/ banned brother. By playing dialectically on the interchangeabiblity of Joseph and Benjamin, the story tells us that the separation between father and son is not, or need not be, the terrible tearing away that the Greek tragedy presents as fateful. Its occurrence and duration serves a precise purpose: it is for the son to discover his independence and maturity, the integrity of his selfhood. As says Susan

Niditch, the novella of Joseph "exhibits qualities of the bildungsroman, the tale of maturation."[19] Within that perspective, Benjamin is Joseph not betrayed and not sold into slavery by his brothers; he is Joseph at home with the father and spared of all tribulations and adventures of an "independent" life. Conversely, Joseph is Benjamin maturing and becoming fully himself through the necessary distanciation from a symbiotic relation that Jacob is only too prone to maintain. The striking absence of Rachel in the story means assuredly the absence of the symbiosis that characterizes the relation mother - young child. Rachel, however, is replaced here by the father who worships Benjamin as he does Joseph. Each of the two sons in turn "fills the horizon" of Jacob, so that he seems not to have other children but those he begot through Rachel, doting on one at a time. With a cruelty that only age and despair excuse, he tells his other children, "My son [Benjamin] shall not go down with you. Now that his brother is dead, he is the only one left" (42.38), a declaration curiously and perhaps pathologically repeated by Judah in his speech to the vizier Joseph (44.20). Thus Joseph's desire to see his brother Benjamin amounts to the contemplation of himself as not-betrayed, not-rejected, not-murdered by his fratricide brothers; in other words Benjamin is Joseph still in the embrace of the father. And Judah, in his address, fully confirms Joseph's intuition.

That is why Joseph places Benjamin above all his other brothers at the banquet table. In the person of Benjamin also is accomplished the initial dream of leadership (37.5 ff.). His receiving "five times as much as all of them" (together?) in 43.34 parallels the prosternation of all before Joseph, even of "your servant our father," in 43.28. There is nothing random in the fact that the royal cup of Joseph is "found" in Benjamin's sack (44.12). Benjamin, of course, is innocent as Joseph was innocent when found "guilty" by his brothers in Canaan. Similarly, Benjamin is threatened by slavery as Joseph was sold as a slave before him. The parallel is so evident that Judah readily draws it in 44.16 ff.

This striking association of Joseph and Benjamin may be sufficient to raise doubt about critical conclusions drawn by some critics regarding Genesis 43. This chapter relates a second trip of the brothers to Egypt, this time with Benjamin. Earlier, the latter stayed at home with his father — a distinct echo of the situation prevailing when Joseph was seventeen and kept at home while his siblings were shepherding at Shechem or elsewhere (37.12). Now the young lad accompanies his elder brothers in their second face to face with the terrible vizier. If one sees in this chapter 43 a later addition[20], that can be mentally more or less discarded as an intruder, it is clear that such a deletion greatly alleviates the reader's uneasiness with the brothers' ordeal organized by Joseph. One feels indeed increasingly wary in the course of the narrative with the protracted trial by Joseph of his brothers. From a literary point of view also, the growing victimization of the brothers by the vizier of Egypt exonerates them of all guilt and makes them appear more and more innocent, even in hindsight.[21] Besides, it unnecessarily delays the scene of recognition (chap. 45).

But one can wonder to what extent such a critical conclusion is itself influenced by modern standards of morality. The point of the text may be different. What some take for a lack of taste on the part of the composer, may be due to traditional literary devices. First, as I said above, s/he may have used *retardation*, so important in Hebrew narrative.[22] That it is stretched here to the limit of the tolerable is not necessarily a flaw of the story, as the films of Alfred Hitchcock demonstrate. The second device, as has been also stressed earlier, is the intended identification of Joseph and Benjamin. It is on the second trip of the brothers to Egypt that this literary contraption reaches its summit.

As a foil of sorts to young Benjamin, Simeon, the second eldest[23] is put by Joseph in prison, thus reiterating the episode of Joseph being thrown into the oubliette by Potiphar. The parallel between Joseph and Simeon is emphasized in the text: Simeon is substitute for Benjamin, himself the alter ego of Joseph. Thus, Simeon as well is put in the position of being representative of another. He too becomes Joseph's alter ego. The difference with Benjamin, however, is that he is Joseph-humiliated, Joseph-betrayed. Benjamin and Simeon are the antipodes between which the whole life of Joseph is wavering. Half way, so to speak, between the one and the other are the rest of the brothers participating in the royal banquet organized by Joseph. And here again, there is identification of others with Joseph, but with an ironic twist: the brothers are extremely uncomfortable, unsure whether the meal marks the end of their torments or the end of their lives (43.33). Their uneasiness puts in sharp relief the contradictory feelings of Joseph caught between poles as remote from each other as heaven and hell.

I submit that Joseph's cruelty towards his brothers reveals the dark side of a person who, afar from the father, can almost at will become a rogue or a saint. That is probably why Jewish traditional exegesis is so critical of Joseph, telling us, for instance, that he was about to succumb to Lady Potiphar's seduction. At the last moment the image of Jacob, as a super-ego, interposed itself, hiding the dame's nudity and that saved Joseph from adultery.

There is between Joseph and father a complex relationship. Jacob's image in the Midrash is not conjured up by Joseph, at least not consciously; it imperatively comes of its own volition and Joseph backs up with fear and perhaps also anger. In this respect there is between father and son a deep difference. While Jacob appears as a "trickster" bending the establishment to serve his personal, even selfish, desires, Joseph is no rebel. He can be cruel and callous (with the Egyptian populace; with his brothers;... with his father [see below]), but he is never deceptive of the establishment. The passage from Jacob's to Joseph's stance, though, proves expensive. The trickster, says S. Niditch, "sees God face to face, whereas the wisdom hero [Joseph] receives his messages through symbolic dreams ... [i. e.] a veiled form of divine communication requiring the skills of mantic wisdom to be understood" (p. 106).

But we need to go one step further. True, Joseph is not the anti-establishment "circumventor" as has always been his father (cf. Gen. 25.26; Hos. 12.3;

Jer. 9.4). But there is a striking exception to the rule. During the protracted trial of his brothers, Joseph leaves behind his own stereotype of "dreadful honesty" (S. Niditch) and adopts for a while the role of cheater. The man of establishment becomes himself a trickster! He also is capable of entrapment; he also can throw the innocent into a pit; he also can produce false evidence ... Joseph's personality would have been severely impaired without these episodes, however painful they may be to the reader's sensitivity. It seems to me that the author's only other choice was to show Joseph committing adultery (as some Jewish traditions suspect that he did). Without one "fall" or the other, Joseph's character is reduced to the static picture of a first communicant. Now, an adulterous Joseph would correspond to nothing said about his father and thus would be "out of character." But a cunning Joseph brings him readily closer to Jacob, and clearly announces a physical closeness about to occur.

Before this occurs, however, a detail of the story that we left aside must be examined. Joseph in Egypt finds himself not only deprived of his father's presence in the land of his exile, but it appears that he *voluntarily* cuts all ties with his earlier existence. Between the moment Joseph is sold as a slave, when he is 17 (see Gen. 37.2), and the time of his confrontation with his brothers in Egypt, no less than 20 years elapse (Gen. 41.46,47). During all that time, Joseph apparently makes no attempt at letting his family know that he is safe and sound, not even when he occupies the second highest position in Egypt! This is certainly one of the most disturbing elements, or rather silences, of the whole story. Is it perhaps a sign of relief on the part of Joseph, who feels that for the first time he can be himself? Or are we to interpret it as a sign that Joseph blamed as much his parents as his siblings for what happened to him in Canaan?

Joseph's marriage with a foreigner (other than a Mesopotamian coming from the "homeland" like the Matriarchs) is probably going in the same direction. Joseph marries an Egyptian woman, daughter of a (pagan) priest. When one thinks of the importance of such an issue in the Jacob saga, it is hard not to see in this a sign a rebellion, especially emphasized in the text by the interpretation given to the names of the children born from that union (41.51 f.: "Manasseh, for ... God has made me forget all my hardship and all my father's house" and "Ephraim, for God has made me fruitful in the land of my misfortunes" [NRSV]). Joseph seems to reproach his father not to have been able to protect him while in Canaan. The long years *incommunicado* in Egypt correspond, in Jacob's saga, to the period when the latter also knew his own exile in the East where he married first Leah and then Rachel, the mother of Joseph.

There is a striking parallel between the two stories. Jacob flees from his brother Esau and also from his father's house; in Mesopotamia, he deals with a father substitute, Laban. Similarly, Joseph, away from home faces other father figures, first Potiphar, then Pharaoh, two contrasting *personae* in Joseph's web of relationships. Jacob and Laban created between them an uncanny atmosphere of total ambiguity. The issue was power. In Joseph's case, there is something of this in Joseph describing himself as a father to Pharaoh (45.8)! This is a sham relationship. To Israel or to Joseph, Egypt is a false substitute, an obstacle, a usurper. Joseph brings Egypt to the total ownership of Pharaoh (47), thus taking an anticipative vengeance, it looks like, on the future slavery of the Hebrews in Egypt. Here perhaps is an ironic forecast of the book of Exodus, when the Egyptians showered the departing Israelites with riches of all kinds on their demand, "and so they plundered the Egyptians" (Ex. 12.36). Be that as it may, it is clearly not to the Egyptians that Joseph is called, ultimately, to be brother and father, but to his own family. As he says at the end of the story, all the preceding events have concurred to the bringing of his family to a land of plenty and to the installing of his father in Goshen (50.20). There, "Joseph *nourishes* his father, his brothers, all the family, their little ones" (47.12; and see 50.21).

The verb `nourish' is stressed in the quoted verse above, for, contrary to what happens in the Oedipus myth, the father-and-son relationship is, for the novella, not fate but opportunity. The accent in the Hebrew tale is not on a deterministic distribution of roles that makes Jacob forever the father of Joseph, and of Joseph forever the son of Jacob. On the contrary, what is emphasized is the dynamism of their relationship and the *reversibility* of their roles. As seen above, Joseph is the "father" of Pharaoh (45.8) as much as Pharaoh is to him a father-figure while he is deprived of the presence of Jacob. So, by being the father of Pharaoh, Joseph is by the same token a potential father to Jacob. He is father of his father, and he demonstrates that much by not only nourishing him, as the texts insist, but even more importantly by being charged with the mission to carry his bones out of Egypt (50.5, see also the following verses; contrast with 49.29). As the parent carries the child, so Joseph, as another Aeneas or St. Christopher brings his father to ultimate fulfillment. Jacob depends upon Joseph as Joseph used to depend upon Jacob.

The matter of Jacob's bones stresses the transitoriness for Israel's consciousness of the Hebrew stay in Egypt . But as regards the relation father - son, it also reveals a dialectic of life and death that need be emphasized here: The presence of the son spells out the imminence and inescapability of death for the father. The new generation pushes out the old. The insistence of the text on the necessity to move the Patriarch's bones from Egypt and transfer them to the Promised Land shows that it is no trivial or romantic detail. Jacob comes *down* to Egypt on the condition not to stay in Egypt. It was necessary for the perpetuation of the Covenant between God and Israel that father and son be reunited (be it in Egypt!), but that reunion of strangers in a strange land is a new stepping stone toward further achievements. Meanwhile, the dialectical relationship of father and son demands that Jacob request, in return of his "dependence" upon Joseph, that the son display his filial loyalty to him (47.29-31). Such a reversibility of roles is again movingly re-emphasized in the description of Joseph bowing before Jacob (48.11-12), as Jacob bowed before Joseph (47.31; cf. 43.28), so that no one can tell who is more important. What more powerful image can there be of the ultimate achievement of a relationship that reaches at that point its *telos?* Father and son recognize in one another the presence of transcendence. Jacob is transfigured in Joseph's eyes; Joseph is transfigured in Jacob's eyes. The continued uneasiness on the part of Jacob's other sons (Gen 50.15-18), serves as a foil to the communion of Joseph with Jacob (and by inference with Benjamin). Between the Great Vizier of Egypt and his siblings remains an ominous after-taste of mistrust, that some day will eventuate in a schism between Israel's tribes. But between father and son, nothing of the kind occurs. We are at the antipode of Oedipus story's end. Joseph does not kill his father, but nourishes him. In a just reciprocity of relationship, the son dotes on his father, as the father doted on the son at the beginning of the count. All potential rivalry is transcended. Perhaps the settlement in a foreign country made the leap towards each other of father and son easier, even possible. At any rate, the terrible ordeal through which Joseph went, and with him Jacob, and with them eventually Joseph's siblings, that ordeal is in hindsight acknowledged as "good." "... You intended to do harm to me, God intended it for good" (50.20).

The novella can conclude. All is accomplished.[24]

BIBLIOGRAPHY OF WORKS CITED:

Robert Alter, *The Art of Biblical Narrative.* New York: Basic Books, 1981.

David E. Bynum, "Themes of the Young Hero in Serbocroatian Oral Epic Tradition" *PMLA* 83 (1968).

Michael V. Fox, *Character and Ideology in the Book of Esther.* Columbia: S.C. U.P., 1991.

W.Lee Humphreys, *Joseph and His Family: A Literary Study.* Columbia: South Carolina University Press, 1988.E. M. McGuire, "A Tale of Son and Father." In Burke O. Long, ed., *Images of Man and God.* Sheffield: Almond Pr., 1981.

Susan Niditch, *Underdogs and Tricksters: A Prelude to Biblical Folklore.* San Francisco: Harper and Row, 1987.

Otto Rank, "The Myth of the Birth of the Hero." *Myth of the Birth of the Hero and Other Writings by Otto Rank,* ed. Philip Freund. New-York: Vintage, 1964.

L. Raglan, *The Hero.* New-York: Vintage, 1956.

Jacques Vermeylen, "Les premières étapes littéraires de la formation du Pentateuque," in *Le Pentateuque en question,* ed. A. de Pury, Geneva: Labor et

Fides, 1989.

J.G. von Hahn, *Sagwissenschaftliche Studien.* Jena: Fr. Mauke, 1876.

C. Westermann, *Genesis 37-50*, Neukirchen-Vluyn: Neukirchener, 1982, E. T.: Minneapolis: Augsburg, 1986.

Dorothy F. Zeligs, *Psychoanalysis and the Bible: A Study in Depth of Seven Leaders*, New York: Bloch, 1974.

Notes and References

1. See below some remarks on Gen. 39.
2. See the development on this literary genre in my *The Feminine Unconventional*, "Esther," esp. p. 56 ff.
3. See Aristotle, *Poetics* 1452a, 24-26.
4. E. M. McGuire, "A Tale of Son and Father," p. 19.
5. As writes C. Westermann, "It is the narrator who is speaking. Only from his lips does the name YHWH fall, never from the lips of any of the actors in chapters 37 - 50." (*Genesis 37-50*, p. 62).
6. The intimate bond between father and son is not unknown either in Greek literature. David E. Bynum calls attention to the *Odyssey*, where between Telemachus and his father there is "a deep connection [...] which made them doubles of each other and required them to share the same patterns of existence" ("Themes of the Young Hero in Serbocroatian Oral Epic Tradition," p. 1302; Quoted by S. Niditch, p. 77).
7. Note that Jacob himself had been the favorite child of his mother.
8. It is how young Joseph appears to modern readers, at any rate. In reality it may be truer to authorial intent to interpret the early episodes in Joseph's life as does S. Niditch (p. 102) speaking of Joseph's "dreadful honesty" that is consistent with his loyalty to Potiphar, as well as to Jacob. Then he is sincere rather than insensitive.
9. There is here a parallel with Joseph's father fleeing away from his brother Esau. The reunion of Joseph with the rest of the family also parallels the reconciliation between Jacob and Esau.
10. S. Niditch, p. 73 (Table 1).
11. J.G. von Hahn, *Sagwissenschaftliche Studien.*
12. O. Rank, "The Myth of the Birth of the Hero."
13. L. Raglan, *The Hero.*
14. With the Joseph story we are again at the antipode of such mythic developments.
15. S. Niditch, p. 76.
16. W.L. Humphreys, *Joseph and His Family: A Literary Study*, p. 76. True, one could attribute the difference in Jacob's personality to the authorial and generic shift from saga to novel. But, Jacob is a literary character, and "through reading, a person is created ... who can then even possess a measure of autonomy and exist apart from the text. The proof is the way that Esther can show up in other Esther stories ... where she says and does quite different things and yet is somehow the same person with a modified personality ..." (*Michael V. Fox, Character and Ideology in the Book of Esther*, p. 7).
17. E.M. McGuire, p. 16.

18. S. Niditch, p. 90.
19. S. Niditch, p. 70.
20. Jacques Vermeylen, e.g., thinks that the second trip to Egypt with Benjamin belongs to E, who added it to the story with the aim of moralizing it, putting, for instance, Reuben in a favorable light. (*Le Pentateuque en question*, pp. 157,160).
21. This assuredly did not pass unnoticed by the biblical author or the final redactor. It was important not to leave the audience under the impression that only the Rachelite tribes were worthy of divine election, while the others were not. A certain exoneration of the guilty party was in order (cf. the attitude of Reuben and Judah in 42.37 and 43.9).
22. Cf. Robert Alter, *The Art of Biblical Narrative.*
23. Dorothy F. Zeligs may be right when she suggests that if Joseph keeps Simeon as a hostage rather the elder brother, Reuben, it is because of the intercession of the latter in behalf of Joseph in Canaan. (*Psychoanalysis and the Bible: A Study in Depth of Seven Leaders*, p. 81).
24. See W.L. Humphreys, p. 130: "They acted in a context shaped by God ... Intended evil is neither excused nor avoided, but is caught up into a larger design that is shaped by divine will for good and life. This is indeed a remarkable balance for any narrative to maintain."

CHAPTER VII

The Perfidy of Corban

Reflections on Aging in Honor of Perry LeFevre

by Graydon F. Snyder

A significant concern of Perry LeFevre was the process of human development especially the latter stages of life. He explored the question of aging in the volume with Carol LeFevre entitled *Aging and the Human Spirit.* Written in appreciation for the contribution of Perry LeFevre to Chicago Theological Seminary and to continue the discussion on aging this article investigates some of biblical roots for understanding the problems of aging.

AGING AND THE STAGES OF DEVELOPMENT

In contrast the more fixed idealism of hellenism, our Jewish heritage understood life as a series of stages, each of which had its function and value. Although one can see the values of aging throughout the Bible, the process has been best expressed in the Mishnah:

> At five years old [one is fit] for the Scripture, at ten years for the Mishnah, at thirteen for [the fulfilling of] the commandments, at fifteen for the Talmud, at eighteen for the bride-chamber, at twenty for pursuing [a calling], at thirty for authority, at forty for discernment, at fifty for counsel, at sixty for to be an elder, at seventy for grey hairs, at eighty for special strength, at ninety for bowed back, and at a hundred a man is as one that has [already] died and passed away and ceased from the world. Pirke Aboth 5, 21

Life is a process and aging is the appropriate culmination of that process. One can sense the function of the elderly throughout the Hebrew Scriptures, especially in stories like that of Job. In the latter stages of his life he was understood as one of the greatest persons of his time:

> There was once a man in the land of Uz whose name was Job. That man was blameless and upright, one who feared God and turned away from evil. There were born to him seven sons and three daughters. He had seven thousand sheep, three thousand camels, five hundred yoke

of oxen, five hundred donkeys, and very many servants; so that this man was the greatest of all the people of the east. His sons used to go and hold feasts in one another's houses in turn; and they would send and invite their three sisters to eat and drink with them. And when the feast days had run their course, Job would send and sanctify them, and he would rise early in the morning and offer burnt offerings according to the number of them all; for Job said, "It may be that my children have sinned, and cursed God in their hearts." This is what Job always did (Job 1:1-5).

Following the destructive trials of God's prosecuting attorney, *satan*, Job nostalgically remembered his earlier days: Oh, that I were as in the months of old, as in the days when God watched over me (Job 29:2). In those days:

"They listened to me, and waited, and kept silence for my counsel.
After I spoke they did not speak again, and my word dropped upon them like dew.
They waited for me as for the rain; they opened their mouths as for the spring rain.
I smiled on them when they had no confidence; and the light of my countenance they did not extinguish.
I chose their way, and sat as chief, and I lived like a king among his troops, like one who comforts mourners (Job 29:21-25).

The Bible was written in an honor oriented society.[1] Honor among one's peers was far more important than rewards. It was the dread of dishonor or shame rather than guilt which obstructed unacceptable behavior. Job was a man of honor, but, in testing Job's faith, *satan* was permitted to take away that honor, that is the process value of aging, itself.

Similarly, older women received the same deference from younger women. In the book of Ruth released her two non-Jewish daughters-in-law from any further dyadic obligation. One woman, Orpah, accepted the release, but Ruth, a non-Jewish heroine, chose rather to honor her mother-in-law by staying with her (Ruth 1:11-18):

So she said, "See, your sister-in-law has gone back to her people and to her gods; return after your sister-in-law." But Ruth said, "Do not press me to leave you or to turn back from following you! Where you go, I will go; Where you lodge, I will lodge; your people shall be my people, and your God my God.
Where you die, I will die—there will I be buried. May the LORD do thus and so to me, and more as well, if even death parts me from you!" When Naomi saw that she was determined to go with her, she said no more to her (Ruth 1:15-18).

To be sure there are some alien voices in the Jewish heritage. Though written by someone in his latter years, the book of Ecclesiastes reflects the most cynical view of aging in the Bible. The author says there is a time for everything — nothing is finally right, nothing good, nothing satisfactory (Ecclesiastes 3:1-9). And aging itself, rather than a process of development, brings days with no fulfillment or satisfaction:

Remember your creator in the days of your youth, before the days of trouble come, and the years draw near when you will say, "I have no pleasure in them"; before the sun and the light and the moon and the stars are darkened and the clouds return with the rain; in the day when the guards of the house tremble, and the strong men are bent, and the women who grind cease working because they are few, and those who look through the windows see dimly; when the doors on the street are shut, and the sound of the grinding is low, and one rises up at the sound of a bird, and all the daughters of song are brought low; when one is afraid of heights, and terrors are in the road; the almond tree blossoms, the grasshopper drags itself along and desire fails; because all must go to their eternal home, and the mourners will go about the streets; before the silver cord is snapped, and the golden bowl is broken, and the pitcher is broken at the fountain, and the wheel broken at the cistern, and the dust returns to the earth as it was, and the breath returns to God who gave it. Vanity of vanities, says the Teacher; all is vanity (Eccl 12:1-8).

In the New Testament we find the same sense of honor and shame connected with aging. Jesus praised the so-called rich young ruler for keeping the social commandments, including giving honor to one's parents (Mark 10:17-22). In the parables sons who failed to express public obedience were certainly problematic. One son took his inheritance and in disgrace and with dishonor to his parents went away to a far country (Luke 15:11-32). Nevertheless, the young man's father accepted him back in honor and with joy. In another parable Jesus tells of a man who had two sons. When it came time for harvest, the father asked one son to do the job. With disgrace and dishonor his son said, "No," but on further reflection did it anyway. Meanwhile, not knowing of the first son's change of heart, the father went to his second son with the same request. In honor the next son said he would do it, but did not. Which one did the will of the father: the shameful son who did what he was asked, or the honorable son who did not? Presumably it was the one who did it, but copyists could never quite accept such a shameful conclusion (see textual apparatus for Matthew 21: 28-32).

One story in the Jesus tradition marks a watershed in the biblical understanding of aging. His opponents accuse him of breaking with the traditions of the elders (in regard to the issue of clean and unclean), an accusation which elicited from Jesus a response rather difficult to understand:

Then he said to them, "You have a fine way of rejecting the commandment of God in order to keep your tradition! For Moses said, 'Honor your father and your mother'; and, 'Whoever speaks evil of father or mother must surely die.' But you say that if anyone tells father or mother, 'Whatever support you might have had from me is Corban' (that is, an offering to God)—then you no longer permit doing anything for a father or mother, thus making void the word of God through your tradition that you have handed on. And you do many things like this" (Mark 7:9-13).

Jesus claims the Jewish leaders have offered an escape clause for children who could and should support their parents in their old age. Indeed they may themselves be living on some of the substance of their parents. In any case it was permissible for persons to pay their vow to God (tithe?) with the resources they should have used to support their parents. The vow apparently was called Corban. The pain was self-evident. In the name of devotion to God and the religious establishment Jews could avoid the honor due their parents. This was serious alteration in the Jewish response to aging. Religious honor could override parental honor!

While one could hardly argue that this passage alone is responsible for the shift in our western world, it does point to a significant problem: honor of parents can be traded for other gains. Chief among these gains could be personal independence from the family of origin. Failing to provide well for one's immediate family would create more shame than the dishonor of failing to provide for one's parents.   The shame felt by children who have "abandoned" their parents makes the plight of the parent, or elderly, even more painful. Consequently in much of American society the latter stages of human development have been abortive. For most there is little honor in old age.

Rather than settle for Corban, those involved in the aging process should consider how honor can be restored to the aging process. Because our society is so much based on law and guilt, such a project will require that those involved in the aging process create a subversive culture — one based on dyadic honor rather than guilt or even individualism.

THE STAGE OF AGING IS ONE OF DEATH AND RESURRECTION

While we are born into a natural family, it is always death which creates secondary families. The Christian act of baptism signifies our death to the natural family and our anticipated inclusion in a new family. In our latter stages of life, death takes on a new meaning. Death does much more than mark the end of past stages of life, loss of past relationships, displacement from past spaces. The new life made available by such a death is what the New Testament calls resurrection. A community of the resurrection will be marked by characteristics visible primarily in this latter stage of life process. Some of them are:

The relationship to previous communities becomes incorruptible

In 2 Corinthians 4-6 Paul argues that death with Christ brings a new life, a new creation. The old mortality becomes swallowed up by this new, real life (5:4). One important aspect of that shift is the purification of prior relationships. One is held in honor, not shame, by natural family and secondary family. Earlier wounds are swallowed up by the new life. We can often see this at times of death when grief shifts to laughter and, by means of positive narrative, the deceased becomes an integral part of the continuing community. Because of this "incorruptible" or "imperishable" (1 Cor. 15:50-53) nature of the death and resurrection stage of life, we conclude that:

a. There should be present in the communities of the aging persons from previous communities who can witness to the individual's purified presence in prior relationships even though now absent from them. Such persons also should be able to understand the aging person in the new stage of development rather than refer back to the previous community in terms of successes, achievement, increased wealth — i.e., values from the previous stage.

b. It should be possible to relate satisfactorily with members of previous communities without necessarily returning to them. A satisfactory quality of relationship with previous communities (In 1 Corinthians Paul calls it incorruptibility or imperishability, but we can think of this new life as one without shame) develops a deep sense of honor. For example in retirement homes provision should be made for residents to entertain their family or others much as they might have in previous years.

Primary dyadic relationships should be developed with peers in the community of death and resurrection

a. Communities of the elderly should help develop dyadic relationships within their own stage of development. We lament the loss of extended family, and, with some justification, seek to retore it. Yet the sense of progressive stages in life recognizes that peers are just as important, if not more so, than families. The child is born in a natural family, but eventually shifts from natural family to secondary family (the church body, for example). For the elderly the constant presence of terminal illness and death itself changes the nature of the dyad.

b. Peer trust in the community of the elderly should be based on death rather than prior life. Such a trust does not expect success, accomplishments, or rewards, but only that people will walk with each other to the edge of life.

Decisions regarding health care for the aging should be made by peers in the community of death and resurrection

a. Authority over the process of life should be left in hands of those who share key dyadic relationships.   This would be true for aging also. Because a person who lives in the death covenant no longer measures life by success, achievement, rewards and longevity, it is absolutely critical that the last stages of life be done with honor in the eyes of significant peers. The person who enters the last stages of life should be understood as one who is living out of the resurrection. It is inappropriate to take such a person from the context of peer relationships in order to save their biological life. Because, at this stage of human development, nothing is more important than the anticipated and present resurrection-life, decisions of placement should not be in the hands of administrators and medical personnel. Family and peers should decide what is honorable, and except in unusual cases, and with the prior consent of the patient, the instructions of this support group should be legally mandatory.

b. Just as it is inappropriate, even ethically wrong, to continue biological life past the point of honor (for example, by using heroic measures), so also it is inappropriate, or even ethically wrong, to remove a person from the process of honor, or resurrection, by means of euthanasia. The individual's pain or life complexity cannot be used to defend removal from the process of life. If the process is to have meaning then it needs to be lived out as completely as possible.

Communities of the elderly should be placed in such a way as to maximize the wisdom of those in the community of death and resurrection.

In so far as possible, communities of the elderly should be located in places where the experience and skill of the elderly can be utilized. The placement of said communities in idyllic, pastoral settings misses the point of development by stages. The aged do not need to be put out to pasture, but, instead, require two things:

a. A place where the elderly can contribute their prior skills and new-found wisdom to ongoing society.

b. A place where inter-generational and inter-capability dyads can be formed. Most obvious are relationships between the elderly and the chronically ill, or the permanently disadvantaged.

Those who belong to life stage of death and resurrection form a corrective counter-culture for an achievement oriented society.

While it may not deeply effect the well being of the aging, the community they form makes an excellent corrective for society at large. A society based on honor and founded on friendship formed at the edge of life's abyss could alter for the better our own values and ambitions.

In conclusion, aging is the appropriate conclusion of a life process. As such it is neither to be rejected or feared. Moreover, allowed to form communities based on honor and dignity, created by a common sense unity at the edge of life, the aging offer to society a living critique, of what is for many a shallow worldview.

NOTES AND REFERENCES

1. David D. Gilmore, ed., *Honor and Shame and Unity of the Mediterranean* (Washington, D.C.: AMA, 1987).

Part III

THEOLOGICAL EDUCATION

In Relation to Our Fellow Human Beings,
We Listen in Order to Speak, to Give Testimony

CHAPTER VIII

The Christian Teacher, Then and Now

by Dorothy C. Bass

Ever since the Apostle Paul warned the Corinthians that "the wisdom of this world is foolishness with God,"[1] understanding the relationship between Christian faith and that which the world calls "higher learning" has been a matter of concern for Christian scholars and teachers. Many have been intrigued by Tertullian's question— "What has Athens to do with Jerusalem, the Academy with the Church?"—and some have even joined him in concluding that "we have no need for curiosity since Jesus Christ, nor for inquiry since the Evangel."[2] Others have forged different answers, ones that allow that the Academy has quite a bit to do with the Church. As a young man, for example, Erasmus urged a friend to "remember Pliny's maxim: all time is lost which you do not devote to study." Later, near death, he rejected his doctor's orders to give up his academic work, saying that in his view "[L]ife at such a price is no life."[3]

In the century since the emergence of the modern research university, the issue of relating faith to higher learning has taken on new shape for Christian teachers and scholars. The powerful epistemologies borne by the university have challenged simple renderings of the faith. In addition, universities and the knowledge they produce have become crucial arbiters of policy and excellence, and thus of morality. A system of higher learning that does not assume compatibility with Christianity has come into being, and with it a new context for reflection on the ancient concern.

The institutional history of this contextual shift can be briefly summarized as consisting of four key periods. During the first third of this century, the research university became the dominant force in American higher education as a whole, while the Protestant colleges that had once dominated the scene sought to live up to the university's standards. These standards—reliance upon professors with PhDs, for example, and the development of specialized departments of study—were often authentically appealing to collegiate educators, though when they were not they could be enforced by newly formed accreditation agencies. The prominent liberal Protestant educator Merrimon Cuninggim later characterized this first period as a time of rapid secularization.[4] It was followed by a second period, one marked by innovative response to the first. Building on earlier experiments, mainline Protestant educators looked beyond denominational colleges as they sought to redefine and reinvigorate the institutional and conceptual forms through which they linked faith to higher learning. The rapid growth of campus ministry, particularly in the postwar decade, was one result; another was the encouragement of faculty reflection on the academic vocation. A third period, which began around 1960, saw the massive expansion of higher education under government sponsorship, as well as the proliferation of programs for the academic study of religion, particularly in public universities.[5]

During the fourth period, which has been upon us since sometime in the 1980s, religion seems to have found a secure place in the academy as an object of academic scrutiny. Apart from this now-pluralistic endeavor, however, mainline Protestantism's accustomed institutional ways of linking Athens and Jerusalem seem to have fallen into disrepair, as campus ministry funding falters and church-related colleges question their identity.[6] Once again, it seems to be time to reflect on Christian faith and the academic vocation.[7] But more of that later.

In 1958, as the activities and insights of the second of these periods were reaching a zenith, Perry LeFevre published a book entitled *The Christian Teacher*.[8] The outgrowth of a series of lectures to a Danforth Foundation Teachers Conference, the book was dedicated to "pioneers in the renaissance of religion in American higher education." The "pioneers" LeFevre had in mind, in addition to Danforth, were the Hazen Foundation, which had supported a series of influential publications and conferences, and two groups related to the National Council of Churches, the Faculty Christian Fellowship and the National Council on Religion in Higher Education. Together, these groups involved an impressive network of thinkers in positive and creative reflection on Christianity's contribution to higher education in the age of the modern university.[9]

LeFevre's contribution to this conversation was, in his own estimation, a series of informal "talks to Christian teachers." Two questions focused his discussion: "What are the Christian teacher's concerns in higher education? [and] What difference does it make in an individual's teaching if he takes both his teaching and his Christian faith seriously?"[10] Relying upon the Protestant conception of vocation, LeFevre identified the Christian motives supporting teachers in their work, as well as the ways in which their efforts supported God's project of overcoming evil with good. Chapters on Christian teachers and the various scholarly disciplines, on pedagogical methods, and on relationships with students and the college community occupied the central pages of the book.

The chapters covered, in one sense, the standard topics of Danforth and

Hazen publications in the 1950s. But LeFevre significantly extended and deepened conversation about these topics by placing them within a coherent vision of the Christian faith, which he believed could provide the basis for the teacher's existential engagement with all of them. The Christian vision he proposed also provided a theological account of how a teacher's work in each area was related to God's transcendent work of creation and redemption.

In *The Christian Teacher*, the human predicament itself is the unavoidable setting of the teacher's efforts. The created and creative goodness of humankind and of the world show forth God's creativeness, perhaps especially in the newness that often breaks out when people are learning together. Yet the evil inherent in society and in ourselves—the doubt, fear, and error that can infuse education as well as other activities—is also a real element within the teacher's world. The vocation of the Christian teacher relies on the involvement of God, as both Creator and Redeemer, in the "teaching-learning process."[11]

A third of a century after LeFevre's book appeared, conversation about the relationship between Christian faith and higher learning is reaching an intensity not seen since that time.[12] During the 1960s and 1970s, attention to this venerable issue was displaced by attention to other theological and ethical concerns. Simultaneously, however, changes in the social configuration of American higher education, which had occasioned the conversation at mid-century, accelerated; higher education itself grew ever larger and more culturally influential, while the churches' role and access shrank. The expanded academic study of religion since 1960 has offered one kind of response to the ancient question about Athens and Jerusalem, but not necessarily a response that provides teachers with a direct way of comprehending how their personal religious commitments contribute to the life of the contemporary academy.

As this conversation emerges in our own time, two approaches seem most prominent. One focuses on institutional alignments, the other on intellectual reconciliations. Both, in my judgment, rely on some dubious assumptions and claims.

The first approach is evident in the current wave of studies, at colleges and in denominations, of what it means for a school to be church-related. Considerations of finances and recruitment seem often to drive such studies, if only because both the schools and the sponsoring church bodies are unsure of how they can serve one another in other ways than these. And in an age of restricted resources, of course, even these forms of mutual service may be limited.

The second approach addresses the apparent epistemological and substantive divisions between the knowledge produced by universities and the knowledge asserted in Christian doctrine. This approach is most visible among conservative Christians, where it has given rise to a number of ongoing seminar-cum-fellowship groups that gather at the annual meetings of various scholarly guilds. In more liberal circles, some of the dialogue between scientists and theologians participates obliquely in this approach as well.

A third approach is possible and, I believe, needed. It is one that would address teachers directly, placing their efforts in a context of personal vocation, existential commitment, and divine purpose, as Perry LeFevre did in 1958. In what follows, I shall try to sketch some of the contours of such a position. In doing so, I extend his insights into a new social context. I also extend the undergirding theology from one of creation and redemption to one that emphasizes God the Spirit.

Let us try to find our way into this approach by considering a contemporary cluster of images, terms, and books that is both suggestive of and different from what I have in mind. Today, many Americans who wish to understand personal vocation, existential commitment, and divine purpose speak not of "faith" but of "spirituality." Some of these seekers are Christian, some are not; some are academics, some are not. A hunger for rich meaning, deep experience, and ethical purpose, all of them difficult to discover in our society, drives their quest.

Among those academic seekers who are in a sense the 1990s versions of LeFevre's Christian teachers, "spirituality" is the defining concept of a number of acclaimed ventures. One thinks, for instance, of the popularity of Parker Palmer's book, *To Know As We Are Known: A Spirituality of Education*,[13] and of the faculty workshops Palmer has been offering around the country. Another important effort seeks to encourage the academic study of spirituality, often in a way that pushes back the normative boundaries of scholarship by incorporating experiential and sapiential modes of research.[14] In addition, major publishing projects that are producing impressive series of books on World Spirituality and American Spirituality signal this widespread interest.[15]

I confess to being one of those who was originally left cold by this emergent interest. (My hunch is that many academics who share my background in the liberal Reformed tradition responded in a similar fashion.) There seem to be three possible reasons for my resistance, as best as I can identify them. First, my home branch of the Christian family tree has emphasized intellectual pursuits on the one hand and social activism on the other. Bearing these emphases into the smug, otherworldly, or fuzzy precincts of American religiosity, we have assumed that people deeply interested in spiritual matters saw the basic content of Christianity differently than we did, as anti-political or anti-intellectual. Later, after the arrival of the "me" decade, the term acquired a second set of negative connotations; spirituality seemed to refer to therapeutic versions of religion, detached from social institutions and indulging apolitical individualism. Perhaps a third reason for discomfort has been the simpler one of denominational culture: much of the interest in and conceptualization of spirituality has emerged from bearers of the Catholic tradition, which has a long history of explicit practical and theological reflection on this subject.

More recently, however, two other factors have led me to revise my estimate and to see considerable value in the term and the reality of spirituality. First, important research on liberation movements, including African-American and Latin American struggles for justice, has emphasized the roots of these movements in popular piety, and their continuing reliance on the spiritual resources of their participants.[16] Such cases make clear that deep interest in spirituality, far from being apolitical and anti-intellectual, can enhance both action and thought. Second, understanding that even middle-class North-American spirituality advocates have honed their position against specific, restrictive ways of knowing and being has enhanced not only my compassion for their effort, but also my assent to some of their claims.[17] The resurgent emphasis on existential and personal religiousness is an important corrective to the definitive supremacy of doctrinal correctness in some confessions and of moral rigidity in others. Indeed, it is not dissimilar to the corrective once borne by the Protestant Reformers.

We are pursuing the idea that this widespread interest in spirituality might suggest fresh ways of thinking about the Christian vocation of the scholar/teacher. This interest gives evidence of hunger, among academics and others, for a deeply appropriated and personally committed approach to our lives and work. To proceed further, however, we need to examine critically one of its central emphases, which Sandra Schneiders calls "the emphasis in spirituality on inclusivity, wholeness, integration, and the validation of experience."[18]

Is "wholeness" what Christian teachers need if we are to live and think in fresh ways about our vocation and its contributions to God's purpose for humankind? As it is usually conceived by the advocates of enhanced spirituality, the idea that what we lack is a wholeness or unity of self derives from a specific way of construing what our problem as human beings is, at its deepest level. It is a solution addressed to a particular problem: the emphasis, particularly in Roman Catholic tradition, on the separation of the body/flesh from the soul/mind/spirit. Even for those rebellious Catholics who now see this analysis as a mistake, the false consciousness the analysis generated remains the defining problem to which "wholeness" provides a helpful corrective. Upon this rests the massive influence of Matthew Fox in the spirituality movement.

For those shaped by other problems, the image of wholeness might seem helpful in addressing separations of other kinds. For instance, many modern academics would be attracted to a wholeness capable of challenging the fragmentation that assigns committee work to Thursday, scholarship to Friday, embodiment to Saturday, and religion to Sunday.

Even so, if we are to arrive at a spirituality capable of grounding a vocation that can be identified as Christian, we must look beyond this image. We will need to explore other ways of thinking about what the human predicament is and about the divine help and hope we are offered as we labor within it. We will need to think not so much about our yearning for wholeness, as about the ways in which we are oriented, whole or not, amidst the mighty forces of evil and good that struggle within us and in our world.

For this, we need not spirituality but the Holy Spirit.

In the early church, the Christian life was inseparable from the presence of the Holy Spirit; indeed, to be a Christian was to have "life in the Spirit." The goodness of such life did not have to do with reuniting problematic human flesh with eternal disembodied spirit; rather, it had to do with receiving a gift of grace and living a life of love. As Paul described it, life in the Spirit touched the believer in personal, existential ways, but it always carried her into community. Unlike life according to the flesh, which was dominated by fear and endless striving, life in the Spirit was confident and free. Its fruit and its sign were love.[19]

What would it mean for Christian teachers to reflect upon the ways in which their practice might be informed by life in the Spirit? A few examples will suggest what sorts of insights might emerge from such a process. Were they to think together in this way, Christian academics would be prodded to see their own accomplishments—publications, tenure, status, and the rest—in far less ultimate terms than they now do. They would be urged to be less fearful of intellectual positions that differed from their own, abandoning what the theologian Edward Farley has called "intellectual life according to the flesh, [which] looks at the world through an unchanging lens, a fixed set of values, or morals, or doctrines, or traditions, [reacting] in fear and panic whenever any of this is questioned." In the classroom, teaching would be characterized by "a freedom toward the material and toward all formulations . . . a never-ceasing lookout for better formulations."[20] As a teacher, the Christian would know herself not to be the students' savior; all burdens and crusades, chosen or imposed, that sought to make her so would be suspect. Yet she would wish to think and act toward the students in love, offering them respectful attention, helping them to resist sloth and error, and setting a tone not just of tolerance but of mutual repentance and forgiveness. Colleagues would receive this love, too.

Thus might awareness of life in the Spirit undergird, form, and reform a Christian teacher's work. To think that she—he— we could attain to the full implications of all (or any) of these insights would seem absurd to one who has confessed to membership in the Reformed branch of Christianity. Yet to live more fully conscious of the life we have been given would itself enhance our openness to the Spirit and our recognition of her fruits, as they can and do emerge in our midst. It would involve us constantly in the venerable practice of discerning the spirits, a form of theology which draws upon the full intellectual, ethical, and spiritual powers of its practitioners, while also subjecting them to the judgment and grace of God. And it would, of course, disclose again and again that we live much of our professional lives according to the flesh, thus prompting us, again and again, to seek the Spirit's help, again and again, in forming and reforming ourselves and our communities for love.

Notes and References

1. I Cor. 3:19, NRSV.
2. Tertullian, quoted in E. Harris Harbison, *The Christian Scholar in the Age of the Reformation* (Grand Rapids, Mich.: William B. Eerdmans, 1983; first published, 1956), p. 1.
3. Erasmus, quoted in *ibid.*, pp. 91, 94.
4. This summary is based upon my "Ministry on the Margin: Protestants and Education," in William R. Hutchison (ed.), *Between the Times: The Travail of the Protestant Establishment in America, 1900-1960* (New York: Cambridge University Press, 1989); see also Merrimon Cuninggim, *The College Seeks Religion* (New Haven: Yale University Press, 1947), pp. 13-14.
5. I discuss these periods in "Revolutions, Quiet and Otherwise: Protestants and Higher Education during the 1960s," in Barbara G. Wheeler, Parker J. Palmer, and James W. Fowler (eds.), *Caring for the Commonweal: Education for Religious and Public Life* (Macon, Ga.: Mercer University Press, 1990).
6. I discuss this period in "Church-Related Colleges," in Jackson W. Carroll and Wade Clark Roof (eds.), *Beyond Establishment: Protestant Identity in a Post-Protestant Age* (Louisville: Westminster/John Knox Press, 1993).
7. See Mark R. Schwehn, *Exiles from Eden: Religion and the Academic Vocation in America* (New York: Oxford University Press, 1992).
8. Perry D. LeFevre, *The Christian Teacher* (New York: Abingdon Press, 1958).
9. I discuss this network in "The Independent Sector and the Educational Strategies of Mainstream Protestantism," in Conrad Cherry and Rowland A. Sherrill (eds.), *Religion, the Independent Sector, and American Culture* (Atlanta: Scholars Press, 1992).
10. LeFevre, *The Christian Teacher*, pp. 7-9.
11. *Ibid.*, pp. 162-63.
12. See, for example, *Daedalus*, issue on religion and education, 117:2 (Spring 1988); and George M. Marsden and Bradley J. Longfield (eds.), *The Secularization of the Academy* (New York: Oxford University Press, 1992).
13. Parker J. Palmer, *To Know As We Are Known: A Spirituality of Education* (San Francisco: Harper and Row, 1983).
14. See, for example, Bradley C. Hanson (ed.), *Modern Christian Spirituality: Methodological and Historical Essays* (Atlanta: Scholars Press, 1990), and particularly its keynote essay, Sandra M. Schneiders, I.H.M., "Spirituality in the Academy."
15. I am thinking of Crossroad Press's *World Spirituality: An Encyclopedic History of the Religious Quest* and Paulist Press's *Sources of American Spirituality.*
16. Many sources could be cited here; evidence of this reality is abundant. So I will name a few examples that are more recent and less well known than others: Lewis V. Baldwin, *To Make the Wounded Whole: The Cultural Legacy of Martin Luther King, Jr.* (Minneapolis: Fortress Press, 1992); Daniel H. Levine, *Popular Voices of Latin American Catholicism* (Princeton: Princeton University Press, 1992); and Robert Inchausti, *The Ignorant Perfection of Ordinary People* (Albany: State University of New York Press, 1991).
17. For example, Joann W. Conn (ed.), *Women's Spirituality: Resources for Christian Development* (New York: Paulist Press, 1986).
18. Schneiders, *op. cit.*, p. 33.
19. This interpretation is based on Edward Farley, "The Work of the Spirit in Christian Education," *Religious Education* 60 (Nov.-Dec., 1965): 427-36, 476.
20. *Ibid.*, 436.

CHAPTER IX

The Appropriate Use of Research in the Doctor of Ministry Program

by William R. Myers

When a Doctor of Ministry class arrives at The Chicago Theological Seminary in September, new students appear to have minimal understanding and considerable anxiety about the role research plays in their D.Min. process. Over the years, instructors from our initial D.Min. Intensive have come to expect that by "research" these students mean, for example, either something vaguely connected with "testing" the "validity" of their sermons or a way they will be asked to evaluate their structuring of Bible study using "control groups" and "pre-and post-tests." For many D.Min. students there seems to be, on the one hand, a curious blend of naive *belief* (that testing will uncover and perhaps "prove" what is the correct practice of ministry); and, on the other hand, *anxiety* that ministry projects intuitively arrived at somehow won't "measure up." In all this, it is a rare thing when a D.Min. student questions the deeper implications undergirding the use of research methodologies borrowed from secular disciplines as they seek to make an adequate discernment about their practice of ministry.

The genius of the seminary's openness to the issues involved in such a discussion is the result of a variety of factors. In speaking about the core of the seminary in the opening essay for this book, W. Widick Schroeder noted that:

> "This liberal theological institution is grounded on three primary values — tolerance for alternative interpretations of the beliefs and practices of the Christian movement, the legitimacy of theological pluralism in its midst, and the right of participants in the community to pursue freely their own modes of theological inquiry" (p. 18).

Schroeder advances his argument by claiming Perry LeFevre as an embodiment of this deeply rooted value; he states: "His commitment to fundamental liberal values is reflected in the care with which he seeks to explore contrasting interpretations of the Christian movement" (p. 24).

It is also clear, according to Schroeder, that LeFevre "focuses more sharply on the empirical side of experience. Persuaded that there is an immanental good more basic than any created goods, he (LeFevre) has sought to identify and to nurture those factors in human life which evoke creative personal and social transformations to counter the evil and the banal in the world" (p. 4). Indeed, LeFevre's presence for more than twenty years as Dean of the Faculty at CTS resulted in a Doctor of Ministry framework open to, and in a real sense, mandating an open discussion about appropriate research methodologies for ministry. Currently the status of this discussion at the seminary regarding research revolves around the presentation of three methodologies that can be said to have certain understandings at their core making them more or less toxic for the practice of ministry; the methodologies include: (1) *Quantitative*; (2) *Qualitative/Ethnographic*; and (3) *Pro-active* styles of research.

QUANTITATIVE RESEARCH METHODOLOGY

A *quantitative* methodology of research attempts to measure available data through a sequence of increasingly sophisticated statistical programs. In this method of research, controlled experiments are often set up in ways that attempt to isolate and measure contrasting sets of variables. Key to such measurement is a true random sample (with equal opportunity for every item) and the identification of experimental and control groups with both submitted to pre- and post-testing. Subjectivity on the part of the researcher is avoided; objectivity is sought. A "clean" design has a sample of sufficient size and can be seen to be replicable; i.e., it can be run again and again. "Control" remains a critical factor throughout this kind of research, and "theory" is front-loaded; that is, a theoretical base must be considered *before* research occurs in order that the researcher can develop a hypothesis, identify variables, and propose an experiment. While it is assumed that this is the best way to do research, it is also recognized that the serendipitous moment occasionally turns what was perceived to be an experiment's "glitch" into pure gold. This style of research leads to articles, for example, like Joseph A. Erickson's, "Adolescent Religious Development and Commitment: A Structural Equation Model of the Role of Family, Peer Group, and Educational Influences," pp. 131-153 in *Journal For The Scientific Study of Religion*, Vol. 31, # 2, June, 1992.

QUALITATIVE/ETHNOGRAPHIC RESEARCH METHODOLOGY

The *ethnographic* (or qualitative) research methodology sets out to describe what can be seen and understood within a culture or a "bounded system" (such as the youth group in a church). In this research, the researcher becomes a "participant/observer," i.e., the researcher steps into the culture or system as someone attempting to discover, name, or uncover that culture's meaning. Critical to such research are those persons from within the system who are willing to share and name what they understand as taking place within the system. Also absolutely essential to this process are the "gatekeepers" (persons who assure access); "key informants," (persons whose words are trusted by the researcher); and the disciplined use of subjective, personally generated data from the researcher's own perspective (via journal, field notes, verbatims of supervisory sessions, etc.). "Good" research assumes data gathered from three dissimilar sources can indicate the emergence of a "generative theme," yet submits such interpretation to critical review from both insiders and outsiders, incorporating their suggestions in any final descriptive picture. Theory is more of a "back-loading" process; i.e., the core of what comes to be understood as "theory" emerges and is grounded within the confluence of researcher and the bounded system under study. A weakness of this style of research occurs when a researcher cannot identify personal assumptions and theoretical biases. While "replicability" is low, researchers assume that a good ethnographic study will rate high in validity; i.e., it adequately describes (like a snapshot) what is going on at a particular moment within a bounded system. Such qualitative research underlies titles, for example, like *Black and White Styles of Youth Ministry: Two Congregations in America* by William R. Myers (New York: Pilgrim Press, 1991).

PRO-ACTIVE RESEARCH METHODOLOGY

The *pro-active* research methodology intentionally engages in transformative activities while interactively working with persons within "bounded systems." A "bounded system" can be a church, a youth group within a church, or a person within a youth group within a church. In such research, the researcher may present "case studies" in which the researcher (and others) are named as pro-active participants in the study. Examples could be drawn from disciplines like psychotherapy where "therapist" and "client" are often understood to be jointly engaged in a transformative process. Research done within such systems relies upon audio and video tapes, extended verbatims, supervisory sessions, the encouragement of introspective "homework" assignments, and the keeping of personal journals. These tools in the research process may be entered into by both the therapist and the client; i.e., the client keeps a journal and the therapist reflects on dreams and verbatims with a supervisor. When the larger community becomes engaged in pro-active research, tools (both quantitative and qualitative) may be "borrowed" from other methodologies. In one sense, whether dealing with individual or communal transformation, the *interview* becomes this methodology's primary tool of assessment.

In addition, because the researcher's generation of subjective data is also respected, the personal journal of the researcher is central to the data gathering process, primarily because pro-active research places high priority on naming and monitoring personal and communal factors while making theory more explicit. Theory is *interactive*, however, emerging not before or after the period of research, but in conjunction with it. A weakness of this methodology is the sometimes strident nature of its reporting; i.e., the posture of advocacy sometimes overwhelms the data with little sense of truth remaining. When pro-active research is done well, however, the reader engages in what is called "naturalistic generalizations" (a term used to describe how each case, once read, sparks comparative responses out of the reader's experience).[1] Pro-active research underlies articles, for example, like "Becoming A Spiritual Director for the Homosexually Oriented Candidate for the Priesthood in the Roman Catholic Tradition of Celibacy" by Thomas J. Byrne, pp. 113-143 in Perry LeFevre and W. Widick Schroeder (edited) *Creative Ministries in Contemporary Christianity* (Chicago: Exploration Press, 1991).

APPROPRIATE RESEARCH METHODOLOGIES FOR MINISTRY

In an article entitled "Can One Be Faithful While Teaching Research Methods to D.Min. Students" (pp. 15-29 in *The Journal of Supervision and Training in Ministry*, Vol. 12, 1990), colleague Bonnie Miller-McLemore and I raised several issues about "appropriate" research methodologies in ministry. We argued that once we had chosen a particular methodology, we had set ourselves (wittingly or unwittingly) upon a course in which the outcome was already, to a stronger degree than what we wished to admit, predetermined. With that thought in mind, let us consider the three methodologies just described. At the risk of oversimplification, researchers who use the quantitative research methodology hope to discover *objective proof*; those who enter the qualitative paradigm hope to *describe contextual meaning*; and those who accept the pro-active researcher stance assume that worlds (both individual and communal) *will be transformed*.[2]

The quantitative research paradigm was birthed through instrumental, scientific reason and a static conception of the world. Quantitative researchers seek the objective facts of social phenomena with little or no interest in the subjective world of individuals. In contrast, instead of seeking to control and predict, the qualitative (or ethnographic) research paradigm seeks to describe subjective understanding (*verstehen*) of the meaning of human behavior from the actor's own frame of reference. As Michael Patton remarks:

> The verstehen approach assumes that the social sciences need methods different from those used in agricultural experimentation and natural science because human beings are different from plants and nuclear particles. The verstehen tradition stresses understanding that focuses on the meaning of human behavior, the context of social interaction, and empathetic understanding based on subjective experience, and the connections between subjective states and behavior. The tradition of verstehen (for understanding) places emphasis on the human capacity to know and understand others through sympathetic introspection and reflection from detailed description and observation.[3]

Thus those who use the qualitative paradigm question the facile transfer of methodologies and epistemologies from the natural sciences to the study of human affairs.

But the pro-active research methodology goes further than the qualitative paradigm's attempt at *description* - instead of describing a phenomenon, it seeks *to stand with* the persons in the phenomenon even as the phenomenon and the persons involved experience the process of transformation. On the face of it, this research methodology is radically different from methodologies one and two, yet sounds congruent with the implications of transformation associated with most Judeo-Christian conceptions of ministry. It more clearly fits, for example, the claim made by most Doctor of Ministry programs when they state that their program is "*for* the practice of ministry in our time." If this is so, we ought to skeptically proceed with methodologies whose underlying values seek "to prove" or "to control" (as does # 1). We must also wonder if a *descriptive* goal, necessarily one step removed from the dynamics of transformation and aimed toward, at best, a "mutual understanding" (as does # 2) goes far enough toward evaluating "what really counts" in the underlying concerns of active ministry.

Another way to put this is to recognize that there necessarily exists a specific connection between the choice of a research methodology and how one comes to "know." Therefore, in D.Min. programs a critical, value-laden evaluative stance is to be honored, not depreciated. A certain critical passion about and investment in one's work becomes a necessity, not a hindrance or limitation. Clarity about and careful reflection upon one's passion, tradition, community — ultimately where one stands — becomes absolutely essential. In such a process, the critical assessment of the implicit norms and traditions of the research models that one adopts becomes equally indispensable. Only on this basis can satisfactory choices be made.

Pragmatically, however, the advocacy stance of our third category — a research methodology that is pro-active and seeks "critical transformation" as a grounding premise — may seem to "fit" ministry and the D.Min. process but tends to put us at odds with contemporary American research traditions (and, concomitantly, with the research methodologies most seminary Ph.D. professors were trained in using). We also need to recognize that, like most seminary professors, the majority of D.Min. students in our schools are American. Because of this they have a singular interest in what can be called the instrumental use of reason; i.e., they want to wed theory and practice in such a way that, through evaluation, they can know how something "works." By such "knowing" they can then control, or minimally, be more intentional in ministry. In Thomas A. Schwandt's words:

> Knowledge in evaluation about ineluctably human affairs (e.g., welfare reform, new school curricula, personnel assessment, medical care, and the like) is knowledge about how things work; to know is somehow to account for some human activity by providing some analytical-reductive

explanation. Such knowledge is potentially powerful because it can be used to direct actions and ultimately achieve desired ends.[4]

The core belief underlying this expectation rests, according to Schwandt, "in the instrumental power of reason and its corollary emphasis on scientific knowledge as the paradigm of understanding." To know, in this sense, is to effectively control. Immersed in the American context, "scientifically informed (if not scientifically managed) social control" appears to be "the ideal" to which many of our D.Min. students aspire.[5] To the extent that the D.Min. degree enhances personal expertise, it often serves to promote a "Lone Ranger" kind of expert "in control" and a privatistic, elitist image of ministry. This model also concentrates authority in the professional and deprives "communities of individuals the ability and eventually the desire to deal with their own problems."[6]

This picture rings true in many areas of ministry today. The minister, whether chaplain, pastoral counselor, religious educator, parish administrator, or youth worker, is first and foremost a "professional" — a "hired gun" or "expert" who "is competent" and "has the tools" to "do ministry." While this misses most of the religious grounding of ministry, many D.Min. programs continue to succumb to these underlying beliefs about their programs and the role research and evaluation plays within them.

TOWARD DISCERNMENT; VALUING RESEARCH AND MINISTRY

Because The Chicago Theological Seminary is a liberal institution, we have seen that while it is open to the use of a wide variety of research methodologies that can be shown to be congruent with specific ministry projects undertaken in its doctoral programs, it assumes that each wedding of methodology with ministry will be accompanied by critical reflection upon value-systems. And this is the critical point - both the research methodology and the research project in ministry have implicit value systems; can such values be made more explicit, and when such explicitness occurs, are the values seen to be congruent with each other? Because *critical reflection* is called for, at the seminary, each of the three research methodologies described above has been considered, accepted, or rejected by students at this institution.[7] Students in the Doctor of Ministry Program, for example, explore whether the values undergirding the quantitative methodology (objectivity, control, measurement, predictability) confirm or override the values underlying and structuring their specific acts of ministry. Another way to phrase this is to ask how the minister as "practical theologian" is called to evaluate a specific "practice of ministry." From the discussion above, we see no clear claim as "practical theologian" can be made if the claims of the theologian are overridden in the evaluation of the act of ministry by the values of the research method.

Attuned to these issues, many Doctor of Ministry students at this institution opt for either the *qualitative/ethnographic* or *pro-active* research methodologies described above. In part, this occurs because the values undergirding these methodologies (subjective "knowing," passionate investment in the "meaning-making process," empathy and openness to "story") are more congruent with the warrants for ministry held by most Doctor of Ministry students. The values of such methodologies therefore seem to be more in tune with the values espoused in ministry, and the tools employed are easily understood by ministers (journals, field notes, interviews, verbatims).[8] But, once the inherent values and goals of the minister/student and of such methodologies have been unpacked and understood, most students move beyond the three methodologies listed above toward what might be called "blended" research methodologies; i.e., students accept as "theirs" the theoretical stance of one particular method and then involve tools from that stance plus one or more tools "'borrowed" from other research methodologies.[9] Such "blends" often have the ability to produce the kind of data sought by the Doctor of Ministry student, but also produce their own kinds of problems.[10] Nevertheless, the "blended" research methodology provides the bulk of what occurs within Doctor of Ministry projects at this institution; and, in that such blending also occurs in most secular research, this trend is not unusual.

Viewed in this more comprehensive fashion (where the values of a given research methodology are understood to play a formative role for the minister and the ministry research project), it becomes clear that a casual approach on the part of either the student or the professor in the choosing of a research methodology may result in a toxic decision unless a critical assessment of both the researcher's and the research methodology's values *for ministry* have been made. Both student and professor must therefore recognize that all research methodologies (including the "blended" methodology) have value-laden, practical consequences for ministry. In addition, professors involved in teaching research methodologies to doctoral students might benefit by understanding such teaching as one of encouraging *discernment* with ministers who are engaged in doing research within ministry. In the understanding of teaching espoused in this article, the professor is called to be more like a "spiritual director" of a "formative process" than like someone who has been hired to simply teach a "statistics course."

CONCLUSION

While the choice of an adequate research methodology has practical consequences that Doctor of Ministry students initially may or may not either understand or, when fully understood want to pursue, a seminary like this one owes a great deal to the informing vision that both encourages the use of many such research methodologies while advocating critical reflection on the values and potential consequences of associating an act of ministry with a particular research methodology. This places a considerable task on student and professor alike, and we owe a debt of gratitude to someone like Perry LeFevre, a person of integrity who has modeled what such a process entails. It is hoped that those who graduate with a Doctor of Ministry degree from this institution have been pressed toward making more explicit their own theology of ministry, and that their appropriate use of a research methodology in an evaluation of an act of ministry is congruent with what they believe.

NOTES AND REFERENCES

1. R.E. Stake, "The Case Study Method in Social Inquiry," *Educational Researcher* 7.No. 3 (1978), p. 7.
2. These fit the typology put forth by Jurgen Habermas in *Knowledge and Human Interests* (Boston: Beacon Press: 1971) pp. 308-311.
3. Michael Quinn Patton, *Qualitative Evaluation Methods* (Beverly Hills: Sage Publications, 1980) p. 45.
4. Thomas A. Schwandt, "Recapturing Moral Discourse in Evaluation," *Education Research* 18, No. 8, (November, 1989), p. 13.
5. *Ibid.*
6. Schwandt, *op. cit.*, p. 15.
7. Such methodologies may be examined for congruency in: Perry LeFevre and W. Widick Schroeder (eds) *Spiritual Nuture and Congregational Development* (Chicago: Exploration Press, 1984); see also Perry LeFevre and W. Widick Schroeder, eds. *Pastoral Care and Liberation Praxis* (Chicago: Exploration Press, 1986); see also Perry LeFevre and W. Widick Schroeder *Creative Ministries in Contemporary Christianity* (Chicago: Exploration Press, 1991).
8. For more on tools like these, check "The Doctorate of Ministry as an Exercise in Practical Theology," *Journal of Supervision and Training in Ministry* 11 (1989):5-24 written by Bonnie Miller-McLemore and William R. Myers.
9. "Blending" has been around for a long time; see, for example, John K. Smith and Louis Heshusius as they write about education evaluation, "Closing Down The Conversation: The End of The Quantitative-Qualitative Debate Among Educational Inquiries," *Educational Researcher* (January, 1986):4-12.
10. One such problem is accepting in uncritical form the "subjective" end of the "subjective - objective" continuum. Another is the lack of *discipline* brought to some evaluation tools, regardless of the methodology involved.

CHAPTER X

Thoughts on a Praxis of Transformative Education

by George F. Cairns

INTRODUCTION

Over the past seven years I have been a part of the Chicago Theological Seminary (CTS) community, first as a student in the M.Div. program and later as a faculty member directing the D.Min. program. One of the exciting and challenging aspects in this association has been to experience an educational process of extraordinary value to me and to many others.   The work of Dr. Perry LeFevre has significantly influenced this process . His examination of the role of educator in theological and philosophical terms has been of importance beyond the seminary community.[1]

What I would like to do here is to examine from both a theological and psychological point of view, some of the most profound changes in learning that human beings can encounter. I will make a preliminary attempt to bridge the gap between what is called "formation" by theologians and what some psychologists and educators label "transformative education". Since I view these labels, "formation" and "transformative education," as simply different professions' labels for the same process, I will use the terms interchangeably. I will attempt a preliminary definition of what I mean by transformative education, then examine some of the "deep spiritual and psychological dynamics" that underlie this process.

TOWARDS A DEFINITION OF TRANSFORMATIVE EDUCATION

Education as Formation:

Along with Merton[2], I believe that all deeply authentic education involves formation. By this I mean that the educational process results in the student's not only accessing an increased range of human experience, but also becoming more fully human. Implied in this theme is that the beginning point of education is not the search for some absolute truth. Rather, as Parker Palmer puts it,

"...the origin of knowledge *is* love. The deepest wellspring of our desire to know is the passion to recreate the organic community in which the world was first created."[3]

I would expand or make more explicit Palmer's notion by arguing that the chief goal of transformative education is to understand and to express healthy relationship within the community of all creation. Many aspects of relationship are extremely difficult to apprehend. Strands within all of the major religious traditions of the world argue that our historical and cultural predispositions make it extremely difficult to fully understand things as they are. These traditions offer ways to clarify our understandings.[4]

One major repository for understandings is the spiritual literature of the mystics. I will not attempt to describe this field of inquiry here. It is far too broad and has been well explored by others. Rather, I would like to examine from a psychological point of view the human experience of transformation that is the focus for such work. In particular, I will examine the process of transformation from the viewpoint of education and learning psychology.

A THEORY OF TRANSFORMATIONAL LEARNING[5]

The Theory of Logical Types: The anthropologist/philosopher Gregory Bateson applied Bertrand Russell's Theory of Logical Types to the concept of learning. His intent, as is mine, is "...that the barriers which divide the various species of behavioral scientists (including transformative educators) can be illuminated..."[6] by such notions. This theory states that:

> "..no class can, in formal or logical discourse, be a member of itself; that a class of classes cannot be one of the classes which are its members; that a thing is not the thing named...Somewhat less obvious is the further assertion of the theory: that a class cannot be one of those items which are correctly classified as non members...Lastly, the theory asserts that if these simple rules of formal discourse are contravened, paradox will be generated and the discourse vitiated."[7]

The theory proposes a hierarchy of more and more abstract classes, with less abstract classes nested within higher order classes. For example, the class "chair" is of one level of logical type, the class "non chair" is of the same level. They are both nested within the logical class furniture which is a class of the classes chair and non chair. If one formally attempts to treat the logical class "furniture" the same as its class members "chair" or "non chair", logical problems arise.

Classes of Learning Types: Bateson applied this notion to describe a set of classes of learning labeled Learning I through Learning III. Each higher class contains within it the lower classes of learning.[8] Let me explain.

Learning I: This is what lay people usually mean by learning. "These are cases where an entity gives at time two a different response from what it gave at time one..."[9] This covers a broad range of learning, from a rat learning which turn to make in a maze to a person learning to play a Bach fugue. With repeated practice, new responses occur. These kinds of learning are often called trial-and-error learning, instrumental learning, or conditioning.

Learning II: This next higher type is learning about learning. "Various terms have been proposed in the literature for various phenomena of this order. 'deutero-learning', 'set learning', 'learning to learn' and 'transfer of learning' may be mentioned."[10] This is learning about the context in which learning takes place. For example, when I first learn to play a piece on the piano, it may take me a long time to play it with few errors. As I continue to play new pieces, the amount of practice it takes to reach the same level of performance will decrease. I have learned to recognize a class of behaviors, "piano playing," and to transfer learned skills from one member of that class, "Bach fugue," to another, "Chopin etude."

As described in more detail below, much of this kind of learning takes place out of awareness. Learned patterns may become more and more generalized and ultimately may color a person's global expectations. The person may then anticipate that the world is mostly punishing or mostly rewarding, structured or unstructured. Bateson argues that these more general relational patterns develop early and also quickly drop out of awareness.[11] He suggests that what is learned is a "...way of *punctuating events.*"[12] What then happens is that we often mold our world to "...fit the expected punctuation."[13] This self-validating process is very difficult to erode because it is out of awareness and the person unconsciously manipulates the environment such that other learning opportunities are missed.

This process can be so general that primary attributes of an individual's personhood result. "In describing individual human beings, both the scientist and the layman commonly resort to adjectives descriptive of 'character'"[14] to denote the results of learning II.

I argue that it is precisely the process of freeing ourselves from these kinds of unconscious patterns that constitutes transformative education. The learning processes that facilitate this freedom are what Bateson calls Learning III. I extend an examination of these processes to include Learning IV.

Learning III: Learning three involves the ability to expand the set of alternatives. Or as Bateson states "Learning III is change in the process of Learning II, e.g., a corrective change in the system of sets of alternatives from which choice is made."[15] It may be described as a powerful shift in perspective or as a breakthrough in understanding. Previously constricted awareness is now unbound, and new ways of understanding are available.

But "...Learning III is likely to be difficult and rare even in human beings. Expectably, it will also be difficult for scientists, who are only human, to imagine or describe this process. But it is claimed that something of this sort does from time to time occur in psychotherapy, religious conversion, and in other sequences in which there is profound reorganization of character."[16]

Learning IV: I would extend our examination to a higher order class of learning, Learning IV, which would have as its primary characteristic the ability to move easily amongst all of the lower levels of learning and, in particular, which would make readily available the multiple shifts in perspective of the sorts described in learning III.

If speaking about Learning III is fraught with difficulty, attempting to describe Learning IV is even more perilous. The very definition of learning IV, developing the ability to cross boundaries of different learning types, suggests that paradoxes and other logical difficulties may, by definition, arise from attempting to capture this phenomena in logical discourse. Put another way, this theory implies that much of the "ineffability" of such "mystical experience" may not lie in the phenomenology of the experience itself. Rather, the difficulty expressing Learning IV experiences in logical discourse reflects an epistemological limitation of what it is to be human.

A *Preliminary definition of transformational learning*: This theory argues that transformational education encourages learning III and IV to occur. That is, transformational learning involves becoming better able to view the world from multiple viewpoints and to shift among these perspectives with increasing skill. This kind of learning has the seemingly paradoxical characteristics of highly focal attention combined with intentional rapid shifts of perspective. The dynamics underlying Learning III and IV are poorly understood by mainstream Western psychology and education. There are hints regarding these dynamics in the contemplative literature from both the East and West. While we will explore a few of these hints below, let us now turn to some living examples of people who have experienced these classes of learning.

Whenever I meet persons who have regularly demonstrated Learning III or IV,(for example master teachers who have formally received certification as in the process of transmission in Buddhism or people like Hattie Williams[17] who demonstrate these understandings through a life of profound service with others), I am struck by the ease with which they live their lives. These persons are fully present on a moment to moment basis and they are able to shift gears dramatically (for example to become fully present to another person, or to a new task) with ease.

In our tradition, Christ provides the perfect example of a person who demonstrated this quality of compassionate presence in all aspects of his life. His life provides us with a norm of someone who demonstrates Learning III and IV. I believe that Christ is also the normative transformative educator, but that is a topic for discussion elsewhere.[18]

Many Christians seek to live their lives "in the imitation of Christ" and saints, past and present. We often fall short in our intentions. Deep dynamic spiritual and psychological processes underlie these ways of living, which are ultimately ways of being. There are stumbling blocks and stepping stones as we learn to become more fully human using Christ and these persons as our normative models. I would now like to examine a few.

STUMBLING BLOCKS TO TRANSFORMATION:

It is the faith stance of many of us in the Christian tradition that openings for deep change are always available to us. Nonetheless, individually and institutionally we close ourselves to such openings. By examining our blocks, we may see ways to increase our possibilities for transformation.

Presuppositions are Critical:

Once we begin a process, it becomes increasingly difficult to change our path. Therefore, we must carefully examine where we start from. I agree with Parker Palmer when he says:

> "But I have come to see that knowledge contains its own morality, that it begins not in neutrality but in a place of passion within the human soul. Depending on the nature of that passion, our knowledge will follow certain courses and head toward certain ends. From the standpoint where it originates in the soul, knowledge assumes a certain trajectory and target—and it will not easily be deflected by ethics once it takes off from that source"[19]

Gregory and Mary Catherine Bateson[20] argue that this dynamic is true of all living systems from individual creatures to cultures. In an earlier work Gregory Bateson urges us to plan very carefully before we begin new endeavors because the behavioral and cognitive inertia that quickly develops from any sustained activity is difficult to deflect.[21]

Unconscious Process and Behavioral Inertia:

Related to this notion of cognitive and behavioral inertia is the paradoxical insight that as we become more expert in a behavior or range of behaviors, the behavior or behavioral class becomes less accessible to conscious awareness.[22] Anyone who has learned a practiced motor act such as playing a musical instrument, dancing, or riding a bicycle has experienced this phenomenon. At first, each minuscule motor movement is in awareness and frequently corrected. Later, the acts become more and more integrated and the small movements drop out of awareness.

I would argue, along with Bateson, that a similar process happens at multiple levels of learning systems. As examples consider the following: individual learning (Bateson's theory of logical/learning types); educational forms[23], classes of concepts,[24][25] and cultural norms[26].

The efficiencies of compression that this process achieves have an obvious significant cost. Since the individual acts are no longer available to conscious reflection, they are very difficult to monitor and change. This causes us immense difficulties including headaches for individuals (often due to "bracing" or unconscious tensing of certain muscle groups, based on past traumatic experience), psychopathology (unconscious repeating of maladaptive patterns of behavior), miseducation (introjecting disempowering educational methods) and damaging cultural presuppositions (automobiles are the only form of transportation for use on public roads[27]). For purposes of this discussion, I will examine only individual and educational psychological issues raised by this notion.

Non congruent Communication:

This problem is exacerbated when non congruent communications are expressed at different levels, particularly when one level of communication is largely or entirely out of awareness.

While studying persons who were labeled as having a particularly disabling disease called schizophrenia, Bateson and his colleagues[28] noted , that certain kinds of multiple message non congruent communications frequently took place between family members and the identified patient (i.e. the person labeled as schizophrenic). These messages involve an injunction, usually punishing " I am punishing you because this is my way of expressing love by my concern for you" accompanied by another message (a sarcastic tone of voice) that contradicts the first. This second message is usually at a more abstract level and may be communicated nonverbally out of awareness.[29]

Similarly, in education, conflicting conscious and unconscious messages are often communicated. Messages that usually are out of awareness are frequently imbedded in the educational methods. Put another way, the communication imbedded in the method is often times masked by the content. For example, requiring massive amounts or highly dense materials to be read in a course tends to push out of awareness other levels of communication. The difficult task at hand captures the attention and other equally or more important messages being communicated recede into the background.

This is not necessarily a negative consequence. However, when the levels of communication are non congruent or in conflict, negative consequences can arise. For example, if I am teaching a class on community development, and my teaching methods erode rather than build community in the class, I do myself and my co-learners a disservice. I am not only mismodeling the content of the course, I am doing it in a way that may make it difficult for others to articulate their dissatisfaction. To the degree that my non congruent message is subtle and out of conscious awareness, by definition, the difficulty accessing it increases.

There are obvious cultural presuppositions in our society regarding race, class, gender, and sexual preference that provide rich grounding for communicating these unconscious non congruent messages. These cultural predispositions occur in our classrooms as well as anywhere else.

STEPPING STONES TO TRANSFORMATION

Congruent Communication:

Gregory and Mary Catherine Bateson call a conversation a "metalogue" when it deals "....with some aspect of mental process in which ideally the interaction exemplifies the subject matter".[30] Establishing such metalogues is one crucial method for encouraging transformational learning because metalogues provide multiple level congruent communication. The educational forms employed at CTS offer excellent opportunities for such metalogues.

Here we do find institutional policy encouraging theology as a practiced endeavor. Here we find the stated goal to apply theological understandings in practical life institutionalized by required courses in field education. What I urge is that we not treat these accomplishments as some bureaucratic or ideological position, but that we continue to examine and improve them in the continued spirit of experimental and experiential practical exploration of our pedagogy.

Importance of Multi-Cultural Education:

At CTS, people from many cultures come together in learning community where we have profound opportunities to learn more from one another than we sometimes grasp. Merton argues that a critical importance of all cross-cultural dialogue is to better understand ourselves, our presuppositions, etc.[31]. This uncovering is less likely to occur without intentional effort to stimulate deepening dialogue. A variety or methods can be of assistance here. One that I have explored elsewhere has developed within the Shalom community.[32] There are many others. Suffice it to say here that I urge us to continue to explore these methods intentionally and intensively.

The Dance of Attention:

Related to the unconscious/conscious nature of all learning is the understanding that all education trains focal attention. Sustained intense focal attention, which by definition pushes other percepts into the background, is an extremely important and frequently underdeveloped human skill.

Mystics like Simone Weil have argued that this outgrowth of the educational process is, in some aspects similar to contemplative prayer and suggests that developing sustained attention will bear fruit in prayer .[33] This notion of prayer as attention directed towards God also suggests how the injunction to pray without ceasing may be understood in an educational context. When this focal attention is combined with the ability to switch the focus rapidly to almost any percept, we have described the perceptual definition of prayer that some observers call enlightenment or satori.

This flexibility of attention is closely linked to Learning IV. Its development is a central focus of many of the Christian mystical traditions. See Jacob Needleman's fascinating work on "intermediate Christianity" [34] which has this issue as a central theme. To the extent that we become fixated at one or a few levels of attention, we again develop the unconscious presuppositions and agendas that Learning II offers. To the extent that we free the attention, that we open the heart, we become more available to the manifold richness surrounding us.

These issues of individual transformation are imbedded in institutional educational forms. Let us now turn our attention to some of these forms and the parallel processes.

Co-Creating Our Agendas:

All academic institutions have certain implicit and explicit covenants among students and faculty. It is a given that we covenant to engage in conversation with a certain body of knowledge, which is really the record of a group of our fellow humans who struggle with aspects of our humanity. The question now arises: how can we create our journey together? First, we must always include our colleagues who are present in the classroom only in the texts. [35] Second, we must contextualize our conversation to reflect the learning community that is present. What this usually means when the process works is that we co-create our syllabus as we go. To quote the priest and activist founder of the Basque Mondragon cooperatives, Don Jose Maria Arizmendiarrieta "We have recognized that theory is necessary, yes, but it is not sufficient: we build the road as we travel." [36] By including in active conversation our colleagues present in the texts, we finesse the usual wicked dualism of content and process that may result in misformulated educational goals. Instead, we view the process as an organic whole with those who have come before guiding and us in our cultural/historical particularity engaging with them to reach incarnated grace-filled understandings.

Tension Between Core Structure and Contextualization:

In many ways, the tension between core educational goals for an institution (most explicitly seen in the curriculum) and contextualization is finessed in a similar way. That is, to the extent that we focus on a particular range of educational goals (preparing one another for the professional ministry, improving the practice of ministry, contributing to the scholarly body of knowledge), we cannot become so diffuse that the threads of this process unravel. Critical to this process is developing some common ground of the sort described below that will provide each of us with extended options while we attend to the "cloud of witnesses" who have come before us.

Finding Common Ground:

One important meta-message to give one another is that we cannot comprehend all of human knowledge. Therefore we need ways to begin our search and set our limits. For example, in a particular course, the way a syllabus is created contains enormously important meta-messages.

One way I have tried to develop congruent meta-messages is to offer a step-function bibliography. Let me explain. Given the time constraints of book ordering, anticipating the covenant between the likely students, and the cloud of witnesses who provide us with the content of the course, and my particular history, I select a few required texts. Then I provide an annotated bibliography of texts I have found helpful and clearly label this list as such. My hope here is that my co-learners see this not as the orthodoxy for the course but to see the interpenetration as my engagement with this body of knowledge as it is played out in my strengths and weaknesses. Finally, I point to the widest set of materials I have been able to find, usually a bibliography of several hundred sources so that they can see the universe of materials, as I understand it. Again, I try to provide access to a broader set of witnesses, not to define the universe for my colleagues. They are encouraged to modify the syllabus at all levels.

I can imagine that, ideally, institutional curricula can develop in similar co-evolving ways. The key is developing the discriminating wisdom to understand how to balance the attention of the community among the fixation points of overcontextualization to the current student body, faculty ranges of skills, the bodies of wisdom covenanted to engage in, and the educational goals of the institution.

SOME CONCLUDING REMARKS

I have attempted to examine briefly how ideas from contemplatives and certain psychologist/philosophers may inform our educational process. I offer them as hypotheses for us to test together. What I have not yet emphasized enough is that all of the above discussion is really about relationships, not things themselves. Learning is about relating to the other in new ways, it is about changed relationships. I hope this paper suggests the multiple levels of communication that take place in single relationships and that it also suggests the multiple levels of parallel, sometimes congruent, sometimes non congruent relationships in which we are all imbedded. If we accept Parker Palmer's premise that the beginning point of all knowledge is love and the desire "...to recreate the organic community in which the world was first created," [37] we are called to be in loving, learning community. My wish is that we continue this magnificent experiment in being human that is the heart of our seminary and in doing so honor our central witnesses such as Dr. Perry LeFevre.

Notes and References

1. Dr. LeFevre has written widely on these topics. A few relevant citations include: *The Christian Teacher*. Nashville: Abingdon Press, 1958.; "Religion and the Teaching of the Humanities," *Religious Education*, LIII, 6, November-December, 1958, pp. 500-505., and; "Religion and the Teaching of the Social Sciences," *Religious Education*, LIV, 1, January-February, 1959., pp. 49-53.

2. For an excellent integration of Merton's scattered insights on issues of education consider Thomas Del Prete's *Thomas Merton: and the Education of the Whole Person*. Birmingham, AL: Religious Education Press, 1990.

3. Parker Palmer, *To Know as We are Known: A Spirituality of Education*. San Francisco: HarperSanFrancisco, 1983, p. 8.

4. For a particularly cogent analysis of the profound impact of these predispositions and ways of undermining them, see Charles T. Tart's *Waking Up: Overcoming the Obstacles to Human Potential*. Boston: New Science Library, 1987.

5. I am indebted to the work of Morris Berman which encouraged me to closely examine Gregory Bateson's ideas regarding education and learning. In particular, his distillation of Bateson's work in *The Reenchantment of the World*. Ithaca, NY: Cornell University Press, 1981, provided me with the basis for many of the insights which follow in this section.

6. Gregory Bateson, *Steps to an Ecology of Mind*. Northvale, NJ: Jason Aronson, 1987, p. 279.

7. Gregory Bateson, *Steps*. p. 280.

8. Here language poses difficulties. "Higher" and "lower" carry much surplus meaning with them with "higher" suggesting "better" or more "spiritual" values and "lower" suggesting "poorer" or more "profane" ones. Not understanding that all levels of learning are always available to us has caused countless suffering and misplaced effort. Just as the class "furniture" is no better or worse than the subclass included within it "chair", so too Learning III and IV are no better or worse than Learning I or II. All are part of the human experience and equally important. It is precisely the *awareness that this is the case* that is difficult for us to profoundly experience and understand.

9. Gregory Bateson, *Steps*. p. 287.

10. Gregory Bateson, *Steps*. pp. 292-293.

11. Gregory Bateson, *Steps*. p. 300.

12. Gregory Bateson, *Steps*, p. 300.

13. Gregory Bateson, *Steps*. p. 301.

14. Gregory Bateson, *Steps*. p. 297.

15. Gregory Bateson, *Steps*. p. 293.

16. Gregory Bateson, *Steps*. p. 301.

17. Hattie Williams was a woman who lived in a neighborhood on the South Side of Chicago that was ravaged by redlining and displacement of people from public housing. She served the community for many years as a caring and compassionate voice for those who were suffering.

18. For one view of Jesus as transformative educator, see Walter Wink's *Jesus' Third Way: Violence and Nonviolence in South Africa*. Santa Cruz, CA: New Society Publishers, 1987.

19. Parker Palmer, *To Know*. p. 7.

20. Gregory Bateson and Mary Catherine Bateson, *Angels Fear: Towards an Epistemology of the Sacred*. New York: Macmillan, 1987, pp.100-109.

21. Gregory Bateson, *Steps*. pp. 292-301.

22. Gregory Bateson, *Steps*. pp. 292-301.

23. Paulo Freire, *Pedagogy of the Oppressed*. New York: Seabury Press, 1970.

24. Michel Foucault, *The Archaeology of Knowledge and the Discourse on Language*. New York: Pantheon Books, 1972.

25. Sharon Welch, *Communities of Resistance and Solidarity: A Feminist Theology of Liberation*. Maryknoll, NY: Orbis Books, 1985.

26. Ivan Illich, *Tools for Conviviality*. New York: Harper Colophon Books, 1973.

27. Ivan Illich, *Tools for Conviviality*. New York: Harper Colophon Books, 1973, pp. 55-56.

28. Gregory Bateson, et. al., *Steps*. pp. 201-227.

29. Gregory Bateson, et. al., *Steps*. pp. 206-207.

30. Gregory Bateson and Mary Catherine Bateson, *Angels Fear*, p. 210.

31 Thomas Del Prete, *Thomas Merton and the Education of the Whole Person*. Birmingham, AL: Religious Education Press, 1990, p. 100.

32. George Cairns, "Establishing Base Communities in Uptown Chicago: Preliminary Reflections on a Ministry," *The Chicago Theological Seminary Register*, LXXXI, 1, 1991, pp. 34-41.

33. Simone Weil, "Reflections on the Right Use of School Studies with a View to the Love of God, " *Waiting for God*, New York: Harper Colophon, 1973, pp. 105-116.

34. Jacob Needleman, *Lost Christianity: A Journey of Rediscovery to the Center of Christian Experience*. Garden City, NY: Doubleday, 1980.

35. I am indebted to Parker Palmer for this insight: Parker Palmer, *To Know*, pp. 54-57.

36. William Whyte and Kathleen Whyte, *Making Mondragon: The Growth and Dynamics of the Worker Cooperative Complex*. Ithaca, NY: ILR Press, Cornell University, 1988, p. 241.

37. Parker Palmer, *To Know*, p. 8.

Notes about the Contributors

All contributors are present or former faculty members of the Chicago Theological Seminary.

Philip A. Anderson is Professor Emeritus of Pastoral Theology.

Dorothy C. Bass is Associate Professor of Church History.

George F. Cairns is Director of the Doctor of Ministry Program.

W. Dow Edgerton is Associate Professor of Ministry.

Theodore W. Jennings is Professor of Constructive Theology.

Andre LaCocque is Professor of Old Testament.

Bonnie J. Miller-McLemore is Associate Professor of Religion, Personality and Culture.

William R. Myers is Professor of Religious Education.

W. Widick Schroeder is Professor of Religion and Society.

Graydon F. Snyder is Professor of New Testament.

Susan Brooks Thistlethwaite is Professor of Theology.

PUBLICATIONS BY PERRY D. LEFEVRE

Books Written

1. *The Prayers of Kierkegaard.* Chicago: University of Chicago Press, 1956. Phoenix paperback 1963. Midway Reprint, 1976.
2. *The Christian Teacher.* Nashville: Abingdon Press, 1958.
3. *Everyday Words.* (with Richard L. Snyder) Boston: Division of Christian Education, Congregational Churches, 1958.
4. *Introduction to Religious Existentialism.* Chicago: University of Chicago Home Study Department, 1960.
5. *Understandings of Man.* Philadelphia: Westminster Press, 1966.
6. *Man: Six Modern Interpretations.* Philadelphia: Geneva Press, 1968. Also translated into Korean.
7. *Conflict in a Voluntary Association.* Chicago Exploration Press, 1981.
8. *Understandings of Prayer.* Philadelphia: Westminster Press, 1981.
9. *Radical Prayer,* Chicago: Exploration Press, 1982.

Books Edited

1. *Philosophical Resources for Christian Thought.* Nashville: Abingdon Press, 1968.
2. *Aging and the Human Spirit.* (with Carol LeFevre) Chicago: Exploration Press, 1981. Second edition 1985.
3. *Paul Tillich. The Meaning of Health.* Chicago: Exploration Press, 1984.
4. *Spiritual Nurture and Congregational Development* (with W.W. Schroeder). Chicago: Exploration Press, 1984.
5. *Daniel Day Williams: Essays in Process Theology.* Chicago: Exploration Press, 1985.
6. *Pastoral Care and Liberation Praxis.* (with W. W. Schroeder) Chicago: Exploration Press, 1985.
7. *Bernard Eugene Meland: Essays in Constructive Theology.* Chicago: Exploration Press, 1988.
8. *Creative Ministries in Contemporary Christianity.* (with W. W. Schroeder). Chicago: Exploration Press, 1991.

Articles

1. "An Experiment in Theological Education," *CTS Register.* March, 1945.
2. "The ABC's of Worship" *CTS Register,* November, 1945.
3. "Student Life 1945-46" *CTS Register,* November, 1946.
4. "On the Boundary," *CTS Register,* November, 1946.
5. "Kierkegaard and His Influence on Contemporary Theology," *Bulletin of Franklin and Marshall College,* May, 1949.
6. "The Vision of the Christian Man," *CTS Register,* January, 1954.
7. "Religion in Higher Education," *Advance,* April 20, 1955.

8. "What Does Christianity Say About Right and Wrong," *Children's Religion*, 17, 7, 5-6.
9. "An Introductory Statement," *Religious Education*, XLI, No. 6, 411.
10. "The Ministry of Self Identity", *CTS Register*, March, 1956.
11. "The Nature of the Church", *Bulletin, Theological Seminary of the Evangelical and Reformed Church*; XXVIII, Reprinted in *Minister's Quarterly*, XIII, 3, October, 1957.
12. "On Being Alone and Being Together," *Children's Religion*, 18, 11 November, 1957, 3-4.
13. "On Being Joyful and Being Sad," *Children's Religion*, 18, 12, December, 1957, 3-4.
14. "On Living in Faith and Living in Fear," *Children's Religion*, 19, 1, January, 1958, 3-4.
15. "On Being Good and Being Evil," *Children's Religion*, 19, 2, February, 1958, 3-4.
16. "On Living on Earth and Living in Heaven," *Children's Religion*, 19, 3, March, 1958, 3-4.
17. "On Living for Glory and Being Meek," *Children's Religion*, 19, 4, April, 1958, 3-4.
18. "On Being Judged and Being Forgiven," *Children's Religion*, 19, 5, May, 1958, 3-4.
19. "On Being Saved and Being Lost," *Children's Religion*, 19, 6, June, 1958, 3-4.
20. "Religion and the Teaching of the Humanities," *Religious Education*, LIII, 6, November-December, 1958. 500-505.
21. "Religion and the Teaching of the Social Sciences," *Religious Education*, LIV 1, January-February, 1959. 49-53.
22. "The Child in the Fellowship," *Church School Worker*, 10.1, September, 1959, 58-60.
23. "Kierkegaard's Search for Meaning." *Christian Advocate*, November 10, 1960.
24. "Freud, the Mind of a Moralist - A Review Article." *Christian Scholar*, XLIII, 4 Winter, 1960, 324-334.
25. "Evolutionary Thought and American Religious Education," *Journal of Religion*, XL 4. October, 1960, 296-308.
26. "Goals for Christian Work With Youth," *Pastoral Psychology*, 11, 109, December, 1960, 12-17.
27. "Heidegger and Buber on Conscience and Guilt," *CTS Register*, LII, 1 January, 1962.
28. "Kierkegaard's Legacy to the 20th Century," *Christian Advocate*, April 25, 1963.
29. "Teaching, Art of," in Kendig Cully, ed. *Westminster Dictionary of Christian Education*. Philadelphia: Westminster Press, 1963, 655-57.

30. "Erikson's Young Man Luther: A Contribution to the Scientific Study of Religion." *Journal for the Scientific Study of Religion*, II, April, 1963, 248-252.

31. "La Theologie Americaine Contemporaine," *Etudes Theologiques et Religiueses*. 38, 2, 1963.

32. "Freedom, Diversity and Decision in the Educational Process," *CTS Register*, October, 1964.

33. "Questions to Martin Buber, in Sidney, Rome," ed. *Philosophical Interrogations*. New York: Holt, Rinehart, 1964, 29-30.

34. "Man of Prayer," *Midway*, No. 17, Winter, 1964, 2-22.

35. "The Christian Concept of Higher Education and the Role of the Professor," *Key News*, IX 5, February-March, 1964.

36. "Teilhard's Vision of Man," *CTS Register*, LV 4, December, 1964.

37. "The Local Church in Crisis," *CTS Register*, 8 June, 1966.

38. "On Being 'With' Another," *CTS Register*, LVII 3, December 1966.

39. "What Are the Psychological Effects of Pre-Marital Intercourse?" *Medical Aspects of Human Sexuality*, II 4, April, 1968, 26.

40. "On Rereading Boisen," *Pastoral Psychology*, 19 186, September, 1968, 4-7, 4-7.

41. "The Snare of Truth" in Peter Homans, ed. *The Dialogue Between Theology and Psychology*. Chicago: University of Chicago Press, 1968, 33-52. Reprinted in *Pastoral Psychology*, 119 187, October, 1968.

42 "Reflections on Teaching Theology in Seminary," *CTS Register*, LVIII 6, September, 1968.

43. "Innovation and Renewal in Theological Education, *Proceedings of the Association for Clinical Pastoral Education*, 1969.

44. "New Models of Theological Education," *Nexus*, XII, 3 Spring, 1969, 25-27.

45. "The Church and Societal Attitudes Toward Old Age," in *Proceedings of Religion and the Elderly in Contemporary Society*, Southwest Center for Gerontological Studies, 1969.

46. "The Hong Translation of Kierkegaard's Papirer," *Journal of Religion*, 50 January, 1970, 69-78.

47. "Experience as a Datum for Theology," in *Proceedings* Association for Professional Education for Ministry, 1972. Reprinted in *CTS Register*, February, 1973.

48. "Life Style as a Religious and Ethical Issue in American Thought," *CTS Register*, Spring, 1976. Reprinted in C. Manschreck and B. Zikmund eds, *The American Religious Experiment*, Chicago: Exploration Press, 1976.

49. "The New Spirituality," *CTS Register*, Spring, 1978. Reprinted in Robert Moore, ed. *Sources of Vitality*, Chicago: Exploration Press, 1979.

50. "On Interpreting Kierkegaard," *Journal of Religion*, 6/11, 1, January, 1981, 88-93.

51. "Commentary on the Hartford Program: *Theological Education* 16 Winter, 1980, Special Issue, 2, 263-65.

52. "Radical Prayer," *CTS Register*, Spring, 1982. Reprinted in *Radical Prayer*, Chicago: Exploration Press, 1982.

53: "Toward a Theology of Aging." *CTS Register*, Fall, 1984. Reprinted in 2nd edition of *Aging and the Human Spirit*.

54. "Charge to the Graduates," *CTS Tower News*, Spring, 1985.

55. "The New Manual on Ministry: Some Theological Reflections," *CTS Register*, LXXVII 3, Fall, 1987, 13-19.

56. "At the Banquet," *CTS Register*, LLXXXVII, 2 Spring, 1987, 29-33.

57. "What Happened to the Theological Vitality," *The Unitarian Universalist Christian*, 42, 4, Winter, 1987, 31-32.

58. "The Right Word," *CTS Tower News*, Spring, 1988.

59. "Christmas is Good News," *UCC Sunday Bulletin*, December 25, 1988.

60. Articles on "Prayer," "Person," "Existentialism and Pastoral Care" in Rodney Hunter, ed. *Dictionary of Pastoral Care and Counseling*, Nashville: Abingdon Press, 1990.

61. "Religious Organizations: Response to Needs," *Journal of Aging and Judaism*, 5, 2 Winter, 1990, 137-40.

62. "Man With A Dream: Shelby Rooks," *New Conversations*, XIV, No. 1, 1991, 15-18.

63. "Daniel Day Williams" in Creighton Peden and Jerome Stone, *Pioneers in Religious Inquiry*, Edwin Mellon Press, forthcoming.